Gong Hee Fot Choy

BOOK of FORTUNE

A fortune-telling Game which uses regular
Playing Cards

includes lessons in Astrology and Numerology

Find your soul age

MARGARETE WARD

CELESTIALARTS

Berkeley, Toronto

Cover image provided by Corrie Grové
Text design by Brad Greene
Clip art from Dover Publications

CELESTIALARTS

PO Box 7123
Berkeley, California 94707

or email us at www.tenspeed.com

Distributed in Australia by Simon and Schuster Australia, in Canada by Ten Speed Press Canada, in New Zealand by Southern Publishers Group, in South Africa by Real Books, and in the United Kingdom and Europe by Airlift Book Company.

Library of Congress Catalog Number on file with the publisher
Printed in Canada

2 3 4 5 6 — 09 08 07 06 05

Table of Contents

A Message to You   1

Directions   3

The Houses   9

How to Find Your Soul Age by Numerology   137

A Lesson in Astrology   139

The Zodiac Signs   143

A Message to You

We were put on this beautiful earth to enjoy it and gain knowledge. This is the Infinite plan. It was not originally intended for us to suffer. Good is positive and bad is the opposite, or negative.

According to *Gong Hee Fot Choy* life holds three to one in favor of good over evil and it is largely a matter of individual concentration and effort as to the success of a personal effort to gain the things which each of us desires.

All are eager to know what the future holds. For this reason most persons, including myself, are curious as to what is beyond the curtain of tomorrow.

As a world traveler I have been constantly interested in what is commonly called "Fortune-telling." Circling the world several times as I have, ample opportunity was afforded me to visit card readers, mystics of almost every country, and to study their methods and the lore behind their art. One of the most interesting studies I made was of the fortune-telling in China, that great ocean of ancient mystic knowledge.

Based on what I have learned through these myriads of experiences I have crystallized my observations into this game of *Gong Hee Fot Choy*—"Greetings of Riches." The inspiration came through the almost innumerable pleas of my friends to have me read their fortune with cards. I did this, morning, noon and night, and days on-end until the demand upon my time became so great that, in justice to all, I decided to place my method at the disposal not only of my intimate friends but the world at large. This I have done in *Gong Hee Fot Choy*.

Power lies within ourselves to possess the good things of life. We must concentrate on the things we want and not fret and worry about them. Few know how to concentrate and also few realize that concentration and worry are two widely different mental actions. For example, my friends see that I am successful in whatever I undertake and ask me, "Why

do you get so much out of life while I have to struggle so hard for everything I obtain?" Of course, I do feel sorry for them and immediately start helping to straighten out life's tangled threads.

By means of *Gong Hee Fot Choy* everyone has what I believe to be an infallible method of concentration and by it each person can discover the road to a better and fuller life. This has been proved through the years I have used *Gong Hee Fot Choy* in guiding myself and others.

During my association with the Chinese in China I came to love them and for the first time in my life I discovered there the true meaning of brotherly love and friendship. This game that I have called *Gong Hee Fot Choy,* which literally translated means "Greeting of Riches," was so designated to give a small token of my appreciation of these marvelous people.

In *Gong Hee Fot Choy* I have drawn the best from all the card mystics in the world, including the Chinese, and have welded this material and improved upon it to such an extent that this method can be declared to be entirely new and different from any other in the world.

—*Margarete Ward*

*Remember this, and also be persuaded of its truth
the future is not in the hands of fate, but in ourselves.*

—Jules Jusserand

Directions

Read these directions entirely before starting to read *Gong Hee Fot Choy*. Since presenting *Gong Hee Fot Choy* as a game, I find the public intensely interested in the language of the cards and that they want to know more about this new and different card reading system, so I am endeavoring in this book to explain it more fully. The cards and the board are used only as a medium to aid in concentration. Spiritually they represent people, things, and events.

Gong Hee Fot Choy consists of a board and book. Regular playing cards are used. From the pack discard the sixes, the fives, the fours, the threes, the twos and the joker. Notice that there are 32 cards used and 32 houses on the board.

(I have used four weeks, the twenty-eight-day lunar month, figuratively to denote time. Four more cards are added, namely: Houses of Compass, Moon, Seasons, Sun, making 32 in all.)

Place the board in front of you, shuffle the cards, and make a wish. Do not cut the cards as this breaks the continuity and sequence of the reading. Now place a card, face up, in each house on the board, starting at top and placing across from left to right.

The HOUSE OF COMPASS is the first on the board. It represents distance and thought, and good vibrations. Thoughts or vibrations travel like wireless waves, and each of us has a perfect sending and receiving set within us. This house tells you the direction from which your good vibrations are coming, and helps you to pick up or understand through concentration messages you will receive while consulting *Gong Hee Fot Choy*.

The next house on the board is the HOUSE OF WISHES, pages 13 to 16 in the book. In all the houses each card is listed separately under its respective suit. Now look at the card you find in the House of Wishes on the board. After identifying the card look in the House of Wishes in the book and you will find its meaning listed under its respective suit. Each house has four units—Hearts, Diamonds, Clubs, Spades. If you receive a message

in the House of Wishes which you think does not coincide with that for or about which you wished, and it seems foreign and meaningless, do not regard this situation lightly or conclude that it does not apply to your wish. Remember you know little or nothing of the changing conditions, circumstances, or influences which are constantly developing to govern your life.

When you receive a message in the House of Wishes that you do not understand, this indicates that you should take special note of this message.

The card that falls in the House of Wishes indicates the condition or circumstances that influence your wish. *Always* check carefully the message that is in the house this card represents. Example, if the seven of diamonds falls in the House of Wishes it represents the House of Success. Check carefully the message you receive in the House of Success as the message may either suggest indirectly or speak very clearly regarding your wish.

A spade in the House of Wishes indicates that an opposing condition, or influence, exists. This might be caused by many things, such as jealousy, envy, hatred, or financial condition. The spade has many meanings, such as the blues, worry, sickness, trouble, intrigue, death, anything of a disagreeable nature.

After you have read the message in the House of Wishes, concentrate on the things and surroundings in your life and see if the message applies to these conditions. If you think it does not or it seems vague, remember there are outside forces influencing your wish that you know nothing about. Hold a firm thought for what you desire. Write the message *Gong Hee Fot Choy* brings to you while consulting it so that you may refer to it during the week. Frequently an apparently meaningless message will unfold itself to you as time advances.

In reading the cards in the remaining houses, follow the procedure used in the House of Wishes.

HOUSE OF SUCCESS: When you get a favorable card in the House of Success do not take it for granted that it means success in everything.

HOUSE OF MOON: There is always a mystery about a beautiful moon, which speaks for lovers. It has much to do with our destiny through life, through those we love or love us, as well as the destiny of the world.

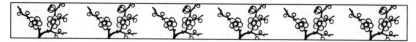

HOUSE OF SEASONS: The House of Seasons represents time. This house has the Queen of Diamonds for its spiritual representative. A season covers a period of three months. The Queen of Diamonds may be read as an old person or spirit and you may interpret in this manner instead of time, also any other face card may be used to represent any one that you may choose.

HOUSE OF LUCK: You may get a spade in the House of Success and in many of the other important houses, but this does not mean you will not be lucky. You may have trouble in love or marriage, lose your job or go broke in business, but while walking the street trying to find a job you may stumble on a roll of bills, or something very valuable lost and receive a big reward. You might buy a ticket on a raffle or lottery, or play the races and win a large amount, this is the meaning of luck.

HOUSE OF SUN: The House of Sun is the last house on the board, and is the house of concentrated thought. The Sun gives light, like the aura or invisible halo that surrounds each of us.

The QUEEN OF CLUBS: Always represents the Inquirer or party that is consulting *Gong Hee Fot Choy,* either male or female, and the house on the board called Inquirer belongs to this card. United they mean spiritually man or woman. When reading the cards always remember the Queen of Clubs represents the person who is having his fortune told, and the House of Inquirer on the board is his personal house.

As you read your fortune try to link the conditions in your life with those conveyed by the cards. When the spades warn you of impending danger or trouble, be on your guard. The same applies to money matters, love and business. There are so many different angles it is impossible in this book to tell exactly what to expect, but with your own affairs in mind, you can very nearly tell what the cards are trying to convey to you.

Also bear in mind when reading the cards that you may receive messages which you are unable to understand. This applies to persons who do not earn the actual money for their livelihood, such as housewives or dependents. Wherever your support comes from these conditions prevail and have something to do with the money you spend and the source of this

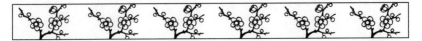

money. So if you get a message you think does not apply to you, it applies to the place of work or business your supply or support comes from. Keep this in mind. Young people sometimes get messages from *Gong Hee Fot Choy* concerning their home conditions or their fathers' or mothers' personal business affairs. *Gong Hee Fot Choy* reaches far into these affairs, and the source of your "Rice," as the Chinese say (we say food). So often they will get messages they do not understand, but the father, mother, or guardian would understand the message if he or she were present at the reading of the cards.

While presenting *Gong Hee Fot Choy* as a game, the aim is to instill in the individual the art of concentration, as concentration is the means whereby we get the good things out of life that are here for us. Worry is confusion; confusion is misdirected thought; misdirected thought is wasted energy. You should know what you need or want, and send your thoughts direct in securing them.

Consult *Gong Hee Fot Choy* once a week only. To consult it more often is likely to confuse your powers of concentration. Do not use *Gong Hee Fot Choy* in a light or haphazard way and expect satisfying results. This cannot be done.

If you want to make a wish for something between readings, shuffle the cards in the usual way and place them on the board as if you were going to read your fortune. Read the message in the House of Wishes only and follow directions by checking the card to get an answer to your wish.

If you will devote a little time to study the meanings of the cards in the House of Wishes, in this book, you can become an expert card reader. **Note:** Each card represents a house on the board, and the names of the card and house are listed together, on every page of the book. Example: ACE OF HEARTS (the abode), etc. In this manner you can refer to the meaning of each card in any house as you progress through the book. As the space is limited I cannot tell you the many meanings of each individual card, but when you read the cards analyze them—read them as broadly as possible. I will analyze the Ace of Hearts. It is called THE ABODE. It represents a home. The home can be a boarding house, hut, hotel, or any place you spend the most of your time. Even an office can be

home to a businessperson. Give each card as many interpretations as possible that have a similar meaning.

Always check the sequences before starting to read the cards, also check your suits to see if many of a kind fall together, like many diamonds, hearts, etc. Several cards of one suit falling together add strength to surrounding cards—and modify the unpleasant meaning of spades near them.

**The HEARTS represent LOVE and FRIENDSHIP;
anything of a personal nature.**

**The DIAMONDS represent FORTUNE and RICHES;
and papers of any kind.**

The CLUBS represent LUCK, WISDOM, and BUSINESS.

The SPADES represent the UNPLEASANT THINGS of life.

Meaning of Card Sequences

4 ACES	indicates a big change in your life
3 ACES	indicates troubles will pass away
4 KINGS	indicates good times coming
3 KINGS	indicates good news brings
4 QUEENS	indicates company
3 QUEENS	indicates a fight or argument with friends
4 JACKS	indicates a relative returns from a distance
3 JACKS	indicates an old friend returns
4 TENS	indicates good luck in money
3 TENS	indicates change of friends
4 NINES	indicates new endeavor
3 NINES	indicates good times in store
4 EIGHTS	indicates change of state, travel
3 EIGHTS	indicates change of state of affairs
4 SEVENS	indicates intrigue, contention, opposition
3 SEVENS	indicates sadness

* This game does not include playing cards—use your own.

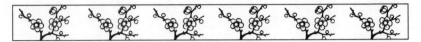

First place the board on the table; shuffle the 32 cards and make a wish while doing so, place them face up, one in each house on the board, starting in the House of Compass, placing the next card in the House of Wishes, covering all the houses in the top row. Continue with the second row, etc., until all houses are covered. Read the message in the House of Compass, using pages 9 to 12 in the book.

The next house on the board is the House of Wishes, whatever card is there you will find listed in its suit on pages 13 or 16 in the book. Follow this procedure throughout the remaining houses.

Two cards of any kind side by side adds strength to their meaning.

Whenever there are three cards, as two reds against one black, it is for the better. Two blacks against one red is for the worse.

Many hearts falling near each other mean happiness. Many diamonds mean success and money. Many clubs mean good business. Many spades mean to guard against sickness, trouble, worry or an accident.

The card sequence may be formed if only the corners touch.

Gong Hee Fot Choy proves there are THREE good chances to one bad in our lives. If we concentrate on what we want in the right way we will surely get it, and when trouble does come our way from the lack of concentration we should handle it firmly and cast it aside. Consult *Gong Hee Fot Choy* once a week and learn to get the good things out of life that are here for you.

Our thought is the key which unlocks the doors of the world.
There is something in us which corresponds to that which is around
us, beneath us, and above us.

—Samuel McCord Crothers

House of Compass

Heart Suit

ACE OF HEARTS (the abode) in the House of Compass indicates someone is thinking of you and wishes they were with you; or the vibration of a new home for you.

KING OF HEARTS (enjoyment) you will enjoy a radio program or you will purchase new recordings.

QUEEN OF HEARTS (friends) loving thoughts are sent to you by friends or relatives. Someone is thinking of you.

JACK OF HEARTS (popularity) if in theatrical work, you will be on the air. If any other profession, you will advertise through a medium that reaches space and distance.

TEN OF HEARTS (marriage or union) if in the business world and merchandising—you will sell goods garnered from a great distance; or you will unite with others in a chain store; or you will unite your services with others.

NINE OF HEARTS (your wish) indicates your wish is vibrating to you in the offing. Concentrate on what you want, then relax.

EIGHT OF HEARTS (moon-love) if single, an admirer or sweetheart is thinking of you or someone that is away is sending thoughts to you. If single, someone is thinking of asking you to marry.

SEVEN OF HEARTS (happiness) indicates you should be happy. If downhearted, cheer up and pick up this vibration. Better days to come.

Sweet is every sound,
Sweeter thy voice, but every sound is sweet;
Myriads of rivulets hurrying thro' the lawn,
The moan of doves in immemorial elms,
And murmuring of innumerable bees.

—William Wordsworth, *Three Years She Grew*

Diamond Suit

ACE OF DIAMONDS (new undertaking) there is a vibration of a new venture around you. Relax and vision that which you would like, then follow the idea that comes to you; or someone is thinking of selecting you to help them. Could be a better position offered.

KING OF DIAMONDS (legal papers) there is the vibration from the spirit world to guide you in health and healing. Help from a physician who has left this plane.

QUEEN OF DIAMONDS (seasons) as this card involves time, it indicates prayers and your wants will be granted, but it takes some time for the things you want to materialize.

JACK OF DIAMONDS (letters) indicates you should use care in sending out hasty thought, for thought in haste, especially thoughts holding back or doubt, are against that which you desire. Always relax and say it is the right thing for me. I shall have it. Never feel I cannot do this or that, because that vibration of can't will surround you. Always feel I will try.

TEN OF DIAMONDS (money) indicates you are vibrating to money this week. Plan this week to increase your income. A prosperous vibration around you.

NINE OF DIAMONDS (surprises) someone is thinking of you and will pay you a visit or call on you.

EIGHT OF DIAMONDS (inheritance) indicates a small amount of money will be received, or someone is thinking of you in favor of a will. The vibration of an inheritance; something to be given you; a need fulfilled.

SEVEN OF DIAMONDS (success) a successful prosperous vibration surrounds you. You use this to put forth the things you want to accomplish. Make plans and carry them through.

Club Suit

ACE OF CLUBS (gift) someone is thinking of giving you a present. They are planning and wondering what you would like. Hold a thought for something you want. They will pick up your thought.

KING OF CLUBS (vocation) there is a vibration of a better condition in your life from the source of your livelihood. Get in tune with this and prosper. Pray and ask—be thankful.

QUEEN OF CLUBS (inquirer) send out a thought strongly in regard to your wish. If it is the best for you it will come true. If there is something better in store, it will be worked out for your benefit.

JACK OF CLUBS (relatives) one of your relatives or dear friends will talk to you about radio work. Also indicates a special message will come to you. News over the air; indicates word of some kind through the air or some kind of work that moves fast—dispatching news, etc.

TEN OF CLUBS (journey) if you travel you will have much of it to do. Many strange rooms are in store. If contemplating a trip you will fly; or you will change homes many times before you are settled. The vibration of change or travel is around you; or you daydream about travel.

NINE OF CLUBS (luck) the vibration around you is lucky. At times you may hear someone express you are a lucky person. Now if luck has not been on your side, repeat to yourself I am a lucky person. This vibration will start working for you.

EIGHT OF CLUBS (achievement) this is a vibration at work for you of business. Work, much to do—encourage it by never putting off that which should be done today.

SEVEN OF CLUBS (messages) someone is thinking of contacting you; or wish you would call them. Relax and see if that person wants to contact you; see if their name will come to you.

Spade Suit

ACE OF SPADES (death) someone that has passed on is trying to contact you. Relax and call to name in silence each person that you love that is on another plane. You will greet them and they will be very happy.

KING OF SPADES (callers) many relatives and friends from the spirit world call on you. Receive them.

QUEEN OF SPADES (gratitude) the vibration of a grateful person is around you. For past favors you will be well paid at a later date.

JACK OF SPADES (compass-thoughts) indicates you will have either a famous flyer in your family or a very close friend; or they will be employed in the media or some work like astronomy; work that reaches space and distance.

TEN OF SPADES (sun) the vibration of sunshine and smiles are around you. Tune into this; it is good for you. There is always sunshine after rain.

NINE OF SPADES (disappointment) there is the vibration of delay around this. Do not be disappointed as there is something better in store for you.

EIGHT OF SPADES (trouble) the vibration of petty annoyances disturb you. Do not let the trifling things of everyday life upset you. Smile and forget; it pays.

SEVEN OF SPADES (health) a health vibration is working for you. Think health and you will be well. Be active, walk—let plenty of fresh air into your home.

> *A thousand trills and quivering sounds in airy circles o'er us fly,*
> *Till, wafted by a gentle breeze,*
> *They faint and languish by degrees,*
> *And at a distance die.*

—Joseph Addison, *Ode for St. Cecilia's Day*

House of Wishes

Heart Suit

ACE OF HEARTS (the abode) in the House of Wishes indicates that someone in the home, or a home condition, or influence has something to do with your wish. Check cards in the House of the Abode; if a heart, diamond, or club is there—a good chance for your wish; a spade—opposition.

KING OF HEARTS (enjoyment) a kindly person or influence will govern your wish, or your wish will be granted through some enjoyable situation. Check card in the House of Enjoyment; if a heart, diamond, or club—a good chance for your wish; a spade—opposition.

QUEEN OF HEARTS (friends or relatives) a friend or relative will influence your wish. Check card in the House of Friends; if a heart, diamond, or club—a good chance for your wish; a spade—opposition.

JACK OF HEARTS (popularity) your wish pertains to or will be influenced by popularity in a business or social way. Check card in the House of Popularity; if a heart, diamond, or club—a good chance for your wish; a spade—opposition.

TEN OF HEARTS (marriage or union) your wish pertains to marriage, either yourself or someone near you, or your wish will be influenced by a union of some kind, friends or business. Check card in the House of Marriage; if a heart, diamond, or club—a good chance for your wish; a spade—opposition.

NINE OF HEARTS (your wish) you will get your wish and sooner than you expected.

EIGHT OF HEARTS (moon-love) your wish pertains to or will be influenced by someone that loves you or you love. Check card in the House of Moon; if a heart, diamond, or club—a good chance for your wish; a spade—opposition.

SEVEN OF HEARTS (happiness) your wish will be influenced by happiness. This card also represents food, drink and entertainment—good times. Check card in the House of Happiness; if a heart, you will get your wish; if a diamond, or club, you will contend with much jealousy; a spade, much opposition.

Diamond Suit

ACE OF DIAMONDS (new undertaking) your wish pertains to or will be influenced by a new undertaking. Check card in the House of Undertaking; if a heart, diamond, or club—a good chance for your wish; a spade—opposition.

KING OF DIAMONDS (legal papers or a professional person) your wish pertains to or will be influenced by a legal matter, court or by a professional person, doctor or lawyer. Check card in the House of Papers; if a heart, diamond, or club—a good chance for your wish; a spade—opposition.

QUEEN OF DIAMONDS (seasons) your wish pertains to or will be influenced by time or an old person. Check card in the House of Seasons; if a heart, diamond, or club—a good chance for your wish; a spade—opposition.

JACK OF DIAMONDS (letters) your wish pertains to or will be influenced by a letter, message, or some other hasty news. Check card in the House of Letters; if a heart, diamond, or club—a good chance for your wish; a spade—opposition.

TEN OF DIAMONDS (money) your wish pertains to or will be influenced by money. Check card in the House of Money; if a heart, diamond, or club—a good chance for your wish; a spade indicates delayed money.

NINE OF DIAMONDS (surprises) your wish pertains to or will be influenced by a surprise. Check card in the House of Surprises; if a heart, diamond, or club—a good chance for your wish; a spade—opposition. The message in the House of Surprises may indicate the kind of surprise to expect.

EIGHT OF DIAMONDS (inheritance) your wish pertains to or will be influenced by an inheritance, something given, or a small sum of money. Check card in the House of Inheritance; if a heart, diamond, or club—a good chance for your wish; a spade—opposition.

SEVEN OF DIAMONDS (success) your wish pertains to or will be influenced by success for yourself or someone else. Check card in the House of Success; if a heart, diamond, or club—a good chance for your wish; a spade—obstacles to overcome.

Club Suit

ACE OF CLUBS (gift) your wish pertains to or will be influenced by a gift or something given. Check card in the House of Gifts; if a heart, diamond, or club—a good chance for your wish; a spade—opposition.

KING OF CLUBS (vocation) your wish pertains to or will be influenced by a vocation or job. Check card in the House of Vocation; if a heart, diamond, or club—a good chance for your wish; a spade—opposition.

QUEEN OF CLUBS (inquirer) your wish is extremely personal. Check card in the House of Inquirer; if a club—you will get your wish; if a heart or diamond—you should take special note of the message you receive in the House of Inquirer; a spade means opposition.

JACK OF CLUBS (relatives) your wish pertains to or will be influenced by a relative, male, female, young or old. Check card in the House of Relatives; if a heart, diamond, or club is there—a good chance for your wish; a spade—opposition.

TEN OF CLUBS (journey) your wish pertains to or will be influenced by a change of some kind or a journey. Check card in the House of Journey; if a heart, diamond, or club is there—a good chance for your wish; a spade—opposition.

NINE OF CLUBS (luck) your wish will be influenced by luck. Check card in the House of Luck; if a club is there, you will get your wish for sure in a short time; a heart or diamond indicates a fair chance for your wish; a spade—opposition.

EIGHT OF CLUBS (achievement and business) your wish pertains to or will be influenced by your own or some other person's achievement, business, or business transaction. Check card in the House of Achievement; if a heart, diamond, or club—a good chance for your wish; a spade—an obstacle.

SEVEN OF CLUBS (messages) your wish pertains to or will be influenced by some type of message, a letter, telephone call, or a ring at the door. Check card in the House of Messages; if a club—you will get your wish; a diamond—you will receive a letter; a heart—you will receive a love letter or a letter from a friend; a spade—a letter with sad or disagreeable news.

Spade Suit

ACE OF SPADES (death) your wish pertains to or will be influenced by one of many meanings: death, divorce, separation, incarceration, love, illicit affairs, or the ending of something disagreeable. Check card in the House of Death; if a heart, diamond, or club—a good chance for your wish; a spade—great opposition.

KING OF SPADES (callers) your wish will be influenced by a caller. Check card in the House of Callers; if a heart, diamond, or club—a good chance for your wish; a spade—great opposition.

QUEEN OF SPADES (gratitude) your wish will be influenced by gratitude or a grateful person. Check card in the House of Gratitude; if a heart, diamond, or club—a good chance for your wish; a spade—great opposition.

JACK OF SPADES (compass-thoughts) your wish will be governed by your thoughts, or thoughts toward you. Check card in the House of Compass; if a heart, diamond, or club—a good chance for your wish; a spade—opposition. This card also means a thief, a young person with bad intentions. Beware of a new acquaintance if unfavorably impressed by him.

TEN OF SPADES (sun) your wish pertains to a desire to obtain facts important to you. Check card in the House of Sun; if a spade—you will find out something disappointing; if a heart, diamond, or club—the facts will be pleasant.

NINE OF SPADES (disappointment) your wish pertains to or is influenced by uncertainty, a disappointment or loss. Check card in the House of Disappointment; if a spade—your wish is very doubtful; any other card—an uncertain condition exists.

EIGHT OF SPADES (trouble) worry or trouble influences your wish. Check card in the House of Trouble; if a spade—your wish is very doubtful; any other card—uncertainty exists.

SEVEN OF SPADES (health) someone's health influences your wish. This card also means—an unsettled or annoying condition or one close to your heart, or a sick-at-heart feeling. A spade in the House of Health—wish doubtful.

House of Success

Heart Suit

ACE OF HEARTS (the abode) in the House of Success indicates that a home condition will influence your future success, or some business transactions at your abode will bring you success, or success in obtaining a new abode.

KING OF HEARTS (enjoyment) your success lies along the line of making others happy. Also, a kindly person may have an influence in your present or future work. You will succeed in work only to your liking. Success and enjoyment are indicated.

QUEEN OF HEARTS (friends) a friend, man or woman, will have some influence with your future success; you will succeed if given half a chance. Professional friends indicated.

JACK OF HEARTS (popularity) your success lies with the public's fancy. Cultivate a pleasing manner and become popular. Also indicates work with fame, or famous people.

TEN OF HEARTS (marriage or union) your success comes through marriage, or your future mate if single. If a breadwinner, in the near future you will gain through the union of some business, either a firm that you work for or the union of some business that you have an interest in; a successful union of some kind.

NINE OF HEARTS (your wish) your wish should meet with success. A successful union is indicated soon.

EIGHT OF HEARTS (moon-love) through the love or esteem of someone you will succeed. You should be well liked if a breadwinner or a housewife; or by your classmates if going to school; or this could be a successful love affair or marriage. Success with love indicated.

SEVEN OF HEARTS (happiness) success lies in an outward manifestation of cheerfulness and friendliness, and you will have to combat much jealousy in order to succeed. Happiness and success indicated.

Diamond Suit

ACE OF DIAMONDS (new undertaking) your success will come through a new undertaking; or bettering your opportunities through study. Something new and better for you soon.

KING OF DIAMONDS (legal papers) your success is connected with legal matters or a court action of some kind. If you attend school, study a profession; that is where your success lies. Successful if signing papers soon.

QUEEN OF DIAMONDS (seasons) time is required to bring you lasting success. Study hard, work hard, and follow the right pursuit. A new proposition in the next three months.

JACK OF DIAMONDS (letters) your success lies along the line of hasty news. Like a mailman or telegraph operator; or some line where news is dispatched, a reporter, etc. Also you may receive hasty news bringing you success. News with financial gain soon.

TEN OF DIAMONDS (money) you will be successful in money matters; you should earn much money in the near future. A large sum of money is indicated soon.

NINE OF DIAMONDS (surprises) you will be surprised at some success that will soon come to you and bring a substantial bit of money. A debt paid or a gift of cash.

EIGHT OF DIAMONDS (inheritance) you will inherit something, a business or shares or a fortune or money collected in some manner that will help you on the road to success, or money collected.

SEVEN OF DIAMONDS (success) you will succeed far beyond your expectations in the near future. This is a positive sign when this card falls in its own house and is the best sign for success you can have. Remember this does not mean success in everything you do or undertake, it is confined to money matters only.

Club Suit

ACE OF CLUBS (gift) a gift of some kind has something to do with your future success; or you will be successful in obtaining a gift you want to give someone, or an offer made to your benefit.

KING OF CLUBS (vocation) you will get into a successful work of some kind; or you will be very successful in what you are doing now. Work and success indicated.

QUEEN OF CLUBS (inquirer) your future will be successful, or that unlooked-for success is coming your way soon. This is in regards to your source of livelihood. A successful career is indicated.

JACK OF CLUBS (relatives) a relative will have something to do with your success, and your success comes through education, or you have a friend or relative who is popular and successful.

TEN OF CLUBS (journey) through a trip or change of some kind you will succeed; or you will get on better if you are your own boss. A successful change near—buying or selling.

NINE OF CLUBS (luck) good luck and success are in store for you; also when things look the darkest you will forge ahead to success. The next nine days should be profitable.

EIGHT OF CLUBS (achievement) if you are working toward some achievement, it will turn out to be successful; you are on the right road or soon will be. Good business or work indicated.

SEVEN OF CLUBS (messages) some message you receive very soon will be successful. If out of work, you will get a position—a salesman, new leads—something along this line. A message comes bringing good news.

> *Failure is often that early morning hour of darkness*
> *which precedes the dawning of the day of success.*

—Leigh Mitchell Hodges

Spade Suit

ACE OF SPADES (death) through the death of someone you will succeed; or some person is dismissed and you get his position; or someone will tell you how to succeed, but their methods are not honorable, or a change of position will be good for you.

KING OF SPADES (callers) a caller will influence your success. This card also indicates the law; you might receive a fine or lose your position or lose a court action. A fine successful person calls on you.

QUEEN OF SPADES (gratitude) someone or some condition retards your success; beware of false promises. A deceitful person may cause trouble, or gratitude shown for help you have given.

JACK OF SPADES (compass-thoughts) an ill-meaning person tries to retard your progress; also you may have to do work you dislike in order to succeed; also someone hopes you will not succeed. If a professional person, media work will be offered—some work that means space and distance. Success there for you.

TEN OF SPADES (sun) through concentration you will overcome all obstacles and succeed. The sun will shine through when things are the darkest, or the sale of real estate or money made through electricity or oil.

NINE OF SPADES (disappointment) you are or will be disappointed in your success or will meet with a setback; or a loss of some kind in financial progress. A delay indicated.

EIGHT OF SPADES (trouble) you must overcome obstacles, worry, and troubles before you succeed. Start something new.

SEVEN OF SPADES (health) your health affects your success; or dismay over success will not help; don't be blue and downhearted. If you don't succeed there is something else for you, or success and good health are in store for you.

House of Moon

Heart Suit

ACE OF HEARTS (the abode) in the House of Moon indicates that you love a good home; or there is much love in your home; or in the future you will have a home with love. A new home indicated.

KING OF HEARTS (enjoyment) the love or esteem of a kindly person will influence your future welfare. You may also look forward to some enjoyable situation, like going to some place of amusement very soon.

QUEEN OF HEARTS (friends) you have a friend, relative, or sweetheart who loves you.

JACK OF HEARTS (popularity) you should be popular among business associates and friends; also admiration from the opposite sex. If single, a new admirer; if married, admiration from a new friend. A new professional friend indicated, a grand person.

TEN OF HEARTS (marriage or union) a new romance if single, and a possible marriage or proposal. If married, a reunion with old friends or relatives; or you will attend the wedding of a dear friend or close relative. A family reunion.

NINE OF HEARTS (your wish) you will be very happy if you get your wish; or through the love or esteem of someone your wish is possible. Future happiness indicated.

EIGHT OF HEARTS (moon-love) if single, your sweetheart loves you truly; if married, the love of your mate or children or someone close to you. If single and you have no sweetheart, a great love affair is imminent.

SEVEN OF HEARTS (happiness) happiness is in store for you; also you will have to contend with jealousy from someone or at home.

Every wish is like a prayer—with God.

—Elizabeth Barrett Browning

Diamond Suit

ACE OF DIAMONDS (new undertaking) if you are single a new undertaking will affect your future; or you will go into some new undertaking that you will love.

KING OF DIAMONDS (legal papers) some legal procedure in court will benefit you socially; or help a friend in court. If an attorney, you will win a case that helps your future; a professional in any capacity, indicates you will do something to help humanity and benefit yourself, or a wedding license will be signed.

QUEEN OF DIAMONDS (seasons) as time goes on love, contentment, and prosperity will enter your life; also before this season has passed, you will make a change for the better. An old lady loves you.

JACK OF DIAMONDS (letters) you will receive a telegram or hasty news from someone who loves you; good news.

TEN OF DIAMONDS (money) love and money should be in your life. If single, a wealthy marriage is indicated; or your mate will prosper as years go by.

NINE OF DIAMONDS (surprises) if you are single you will be surprised, as a certain party you least expect will declare his love for you, or someone—a source you little expect—will defend your character when you do not know it. A happy surprise for you.

EIGHT OF DIAMONDS (inheritance) love and inheritance should be your lot; a very nice combination for this card to fall here, or a gift of money.

SEVEN OF DIAMONDS (success) your life should be very successful through the love of one or many people; or you will be successful in love.

Club Suit

ACE OF CLUBS (gift) you will receive a gift from someone who loves you; or you will give someone you love a gift—might be an engagement ring if single; or an offer made in a business deal.

KING OF CLUBS (vocation) through some business associate, you will be employed, and you will like the position very much. If unemployed, you will do something to your liking, or work for those you love.

QUEEN OF CLUBS (inquirer) someone admires you very much; or your friends admire you. There is love here for you from some source. If single, a serious love affair.

JACK OF CLUBS (relatives) you are the favorite of some relative; or you have the love of a friend, sweetheart, or spouse who will become famous.

TEN OF CLUBS (journey) you go on a trip, you will love it. If single, a honeymoon trip or an outing with your sweetheart; or a trip that betters your condition. A better position will be offered—make the change.

NINE OF CLUBS (luck) you should be lucky in love; or the people who love you bring you luck. Good luck in store for you.

EIGHT OF CLUBS (achievement) your romance may be like a business proposition—to achieve something; or love will come with business; or an offer of marriage if single. Love and business are mixed here.

SEVEN OF CLUBS (messages) you will receive a love message or you will deliver a love message to a friend; or you will talk to a loved one over the phone.

We desire nothing so much as what we ought to have.

—Pubilius Syrus

Spade Suit

ACE OF SPADES (death) someone will call and make love to you; be careful of someone making improper advances, or you will be insulted.

KING OF SPADES (callers) someone calls who should not be trusted; or a disagreement; or a lover's quarrel; or police are called in the neighborhood to settle a quarrel between husband and wife; or a romance with someone who wears a uniform.

QUEEN OF SPADES (gratitude) a mean woman will cause trouble by taking your sweetheart from you; or some mean woman may cause trouble between married people; or an ungrateful person you have helped causes trouble; or one you love is ungrateful.

JACK OF SPADES (compass-thoughts) a new acquaintance holds jealous thoughts about you; be careful, for this person will pretend to be your friend. If single, your sweetheart is thinking of you.

TEN OF SPADES (sun) the sun affects your finding out what you want to know about someone for whom you care; your thoughts will penetrate the thing you are to find out. Sunshine comes in to your life through love.

NINE OF SPADES (disappointment) you are or will be disappointed in love or in a close friend; also indicates a divorce or broken engagement. A loved one is moving away or is delayed in returning.

EIGHT OF SPADES (trouble) the love of someone has been worrying or troubling you; or someone you love is ill or has been lost through death; or you are afraid you will lose a loved one; or a quarrel.

SEVEN OF SPADES (health) you are blue over the ill health of someone you love; or you are blue over love.

House of Surprises

Heart Suit

ACE OF HEARTS (the abode) in the House of Surprises indicates that a surprise comes concerning the home or place of abode. A pleasant surprise. Could be a new home bought.

KING OF HEARTS (enjoyment) a kindly person surprises you. A good surprise. A nice present for you.

QUEEN OF HEARTS (friends) a good surprise from a friend or relative. A surprise party is planned for you.

JACK OF HEARTS (popularity) you will hear something about yourself that pleases you. If single, an invitation from a new admirer. A romance with a famous person.

TEN OF HEARTS (marriage or union) you will be surprised about someone's elopement or marriage, or a surprise party will be held in your honor; a union with old friends. If a businessperson, you will be surprised over the union of some business affair that will be of some benefit to you; or a surprise about an old person's wedding.

NINE OF HEARTS (your wish) a surprise is connected with your wish. A good surprise.

EIGHT OF HEARTS (moon-love) you will have a pleasant surprise about someone telling you how much they care for you or showing their love through action or deed.

SEVEN OF HEARTS (happiness) happiness is in store for you, like a surprise party. Beware of jealousy among your friends. Good news soon.

> *To wonder at nothing when it happens; to consider nothing impossible before it has come to pass.*
>
> —Cicero

Diamond Suit

ACE OF DIAMONDS (new undertaking) you will be very surprised at a new undertaking that comes your way; or an offer made for your services. A new business proposition offered—go in and try it.

KING OF DIAMONDS (legal papers) you will be surprised at some legal action that comes up; you may inherit and require the services of an attorney; or you will have a surprise from a professional person. You will sign a paper like a contract.

QUEEN OF DIAMONDS (seasons) before this year has passed you will be surprised by a relative—something that will benefit you financially. Also a great change in your life will come this year.

JACK OF DIAMONDS (letters) you will be surprised very soon over hasty news you receive, like an old person's wedding; or you will get a letter from a person you never thought would write to you.

TEN OF DIAMONDS (money) you have in store for you a big surprise in regards to quite a sum of money that you will receive soon. A gift of money.

NINE OF DIAMONDS (surprises) you will have one of the biggest surprises of your life. A good surprise.

EIGHT OF DIAMONDS (inheritance) you will be surprised about a small amount of money you will receive, like a loan paid that you did not expect; or a legacy left from someone that you never thought possible. A big surprise over money.

SEVEN OF DIAMONDS (success) very soon you will succeed in getting something you want; such as work or being able to buy something you desire. Also something comes your way that helps you to succeed.

Club Suit

ACE OF CLUBS (gift) you will be surprised over a gift you receive; something you never expected; or an offer made for your services—or a raise in position or salary.

KING OF CLUBS (vocation) you will encounter a surprise in whatever you are doing or from the source of your livelihood. Prepare for a happy surprise.

QUEEN OF CLUBS (inquirer) you are due for a great surprise; get ready for it. A good surprise.

JACK OF CLUBS (relatives) a relative or close friend will surprise you. They will call from a distance.

TEN OF CLUBS (journey) you will be surprised over a change of some kind you make; or an invitation for a short trip to the beach or country. Or an offer made to take you to see some real estate.

NINE OF CLUBS (luck) you will be surprised over some good luck that comes your way; it will come in whatever you are doing, whether attending school, working, or in a business way. Good luck soon.

EIGHT OF CLUBS (achievement) there is a surprise over some achievement you will accomplish, an offer of steady employment. This card connects a surprise and business, so look for something like that to happen. You may work for several people in one firm.

SEVEN OF CLUBS (messages) you will be surprised over a message you receive from someone you never thought would call. A phone call soon.

> *But surprises are like poppies spread:*
> *You seize the flower its bloom is shed;*
> *Or like the snow falls in the river,*
> *A moment white—then melts forever.*

—Robert Burns

Spade Suit

ACE OF SPADES (death) you will be surprised over a death you hear about; or the divorce of a friend—or a disagreeable condition ends.

KING OF SPADES (callers) you have a surprise from a caller, maybe a policeman or fireman selling tickets to a ball; or a tax collector; or collector of some kind; or an ex-sweetheart calls. Something you resent.

QUEEN OF SPADES (gratitude) you will be surprised at an ungrateful person you have helped; you will meet with ingratitude.

JACK OF SPADES (compass-thoughts) you will be surprised over the actions or thoughts expressed by someone you regard as a friend; or news over radio or TV that you are waiting to hear.

TEN OF SPADES (sun) you will find out something in late afternoon that will surprise you about someone you trusted and thought your friend. Be careful to whom you tell secrets.

NINE OF SPADES (disappointment) you will have a surprise over a loss— an unpleasant surprise, like gossip; or an underhanded deal from a trusted person, or a delayed business deal.

EIGHT OF SPADES (trouble) a disagreeable surprise that causes trouble, or that you worry about. Do not worry. Avoid angry words.

SEVEN OF SPADES (health) you will get a surprise that will make you sick; or you will be surprised when you hear of the illness of someone dear to you. Relax—do not be disturbed—it will pass by soon.

House of Popularity

Heart Suit

ACE OF HEARTS (the abode) in the House of Popularity indicates that if you are a homemaker, you will be popular among your friends; or your present or future home will be a popular place; or you will have many offers to sell property.

KING OF HEARTS (enjoyment) you should be popular through entertaining your friends, or you will receive many invitations by being popular. Happiness in store.

QUEEN OF HEARTS (friends) you are popular among your friends and relatives. You, or one of your family or close friend will be famous.

JACK OF HEARTS (popularity) you should rise to fame's greatest heights if you are in the professional world. If in any line of endeavor, you should not want for popularity. Famous work indicated.

TEN OF HEARTS (marriage or union) you should become very popular through marriage, or through the organization of something like club or philanthropic work; or you will work for a well known firm or famous people.

NINE OF HEARTS (your wish) your popularity will influence your wish.

EIGHT OF HEARTS (moon-love) you have many admirers and people should love and highly esteem you. Fame and love for you.

SEVEN OF HEARTS (happiness) you should be very popular through an outward manifestation of happiness, or you have a sunny disposition. Happiness through famous friends. Also it is a warning that you will have to contend with much jealousy by being popular.

To some new popularity
Enjoying none themselves,
They are prone to suspect
The validity of those attainments
Which command it.

—Unknown

Diamond Suit

ACE OF DIAMONDS (new undertaking) through your being liked, you will be offered a new position or something along the line of business; or your business will prosper. This should happen very soon and applies to anyone getting this card.

KING OF DIAMONDS (legal papers) you should have some professional friends; also if you are a professional person or studying to be one, you will become popular and succeed; or gain fame through professional work, or theatre; or in a line of endeavor where you do something or your merchandise could be copied, you will have a lawsuit over it for infringement.

QUEEN OF DIAMONDS (seasons) you will be popular as long as you do financially for others, or time brings fame and fortune.

JACK OF DIAMONDS (letters) you will receive news about yourself or something pertaining to you, like a newspaper account or advertising; or a letter bearing an important paper or contract.

TEN OF DIAMONDS (money) being well liked and popular, you can expect money through this source or money from merchandise or investment. If a professional person, money comes through being popular, and you sign a contract.

NINE OF DIAMONDS (surprises) you will be surprised about nice things that will be said about something you do; or you will be asked to do something through being popular that you did not expect. A surprise from a famous person.

EIGHT OF DIAMONDS (inheritance) because you are popular and deserving, someone will give you something; or by being a popular student, honors will be bestowed upon you. You may win a small amount of money on an advertising program.

SEVEN OF DIAMONDS (success) your future success depends on how efficient you are in your line of endeavor; success and popularity go together. If you work in a professional world—fame and plenty of work are in store. Doctor, actor, lawyer—any kind of professional work.

Club Suit

ACE OF CLUBS (gift) through something you do or because you are popular, you will receive a beautiful gift; or you will be associated with famous people. A fine proposal.

KING OF CLUBS (vocation) by being popular and well liked, you will get work, business, or a promotion; or your services will be desired in some other capacity; or you will work with professional people.

QUEEN OF CLUBS (inquirer) popularity comes to you when you least expect it; or something you do or make will become very popular and be in great demand.

JACK OF CLUBS (relatives) you should have a very famous relative; or through the help of some relative, you will become very popular. If single, your marriage will be very good.

TEN OF CLUBS (journey) by being popular, you make a change of some kind; or through a popularity contest, you will be awarded a trip; or a scholarship away from home. A change of condition for the better.

NINE OF CLUBS (luck) you will be lucky in being well thought of, and if you take an active part in social functions, you will meet people and make connections that will be lucky for you. Popularity and good luck are in store for you.

EIGHT OF CLUBS (achievement) through some achievement or work or business you will become well known; looks like publicity comes to you, or your business will grow—or a better position offered.

SEVEN OF CLUBS (messages) your services will be sought after; or a fine position or proposition offered—written or phoned; you will receive many messages or phone calls because you will be popular with your friends.

> *Yes that is true and something more:*
> *You'd find where'er you roam,*
> *That marble floors and guilded walls*
> *Can never make a home.*

—Henry van Dyke

Spade Suit

ACE OF SPADES (death) you will hear of the death of a famous person; or how they lost their popularity with the public; or if you are popular, you may lose your drawing power or good name; or through a change in business or position new popularity comes to you; or the ending of a disagreeable situation.

KING OF SPADES (callers) a caller will brag how popular he is; or he will end up by asking for the loan of some money; or famous people will call on you.

QUEEN OF SPADES (gratitude) you can expect someone to talk about you who should show gratitude for favors you have done for him. Avoid those you distrust.

JACK OF SPADES (compass-thoughts) a deceitful person will be nice to your face and criticize your back; beware of trouble with this person. If you are a professional person you will be famous with the public. Looks like work in the media for you.

TEN OF SPADES (sun) the sun uncovers deceit and lies, and if someone tries to get credit for something, your rightful place will be established; or you will have many real admirers. If in professional world, the sun will shine bright for you.

NINE OF SPADES (disappointment) you will lose your popularity by your actions, retirement, drink, or a shady deal; or you are delayed in getting something you want. A short delay.

EIGHT OF SPADES (trouble) you will get into trouble through popularity; or you worry about not being well liked. Trouble with a noted person; or angry words with an aggressive person.

SEVEN OF SPADES (health) you will be sick at heart over something said about you; or your health affects your popularity through being a popular athlete, or by being popular in outdoor sports. Cheer up, better days ahead.

House of Abode

Heart Suit

ACE OF HEARTS (the abode) in the House of Abode indicates that you love a good home and beautiful surroundings; and also, your next move will be a better home; or you add improvements to your home or property.

KING OF HEARTS (enjoyment) you will get or have had great enjoyment from your home life through the efforts of some kindly person; or a mortgage paid through the help of an older person.

QUEEN OF HEARTS (friends) through a friend you will have or obtain a home. Friendly help for you.

JACK OF HEARTS (popularity) your home will become popular through kindness that is shown to callers; or you will purchase a fine piece of property that will be of great value later.

TEN OF HEARTS (marriage or union) a wedding may take place in your home; or some relatives or friends will come to visit you, making a family reunion. Good time indicated.

NINE OF HEARTS (your wish) your wish has something to do with a condition in the home. You should get your wish.

EIGHT OF HEARTS (moon-love) before many moons pass you can expect the joys of a new home—one you will love—if you haven't the new home now.

SEVEN OF HEARTS (happiness) you will overcome difficulties sometime in your life obtaining a home, which will give you much happiness. You may have to contend with much jealousy where you live. If you have a home you will improve it.

> But every house where love abides
> And friendship is a guest
> Is surely home, and home, sweet home;
> For there the heart can rest.

> —Henry van Dyke

Diamond Suit

ACE OF DIAMONDS (new undertaking) money will be spent in the home to a good advantage; or you are contemplating buying a home; or some new undertaking will start in the home and should meet with success; or the starting of a new business.

KING OF DIAMONDS (legal papers) if you are a doctor, or in any other line of healing, you will have patients calling where you live; or your home should have some influence of a professional person; or you will have an attorney visit your home in regards to some legal papers or action; or you will buy or sell property.

QUEEN OF DIAMONDS (seasons) there is a big change coming into your home for the best before this season has passed.

JACK OF DIAMONDS (letters) you can expect hasty news to be delivered to your home soon, a telegram or long-distance call or airmail letter; or news pertaining to property. Good news.

TEN OF DIAMONDS (money) sometime in your life you will own your own home, and it will be well furnished; or money will come through some endeavor in the home; or you sell property for a substantial sum.

NINE OF DIAMONDS (surprises) a big surprise comes into your home; a good surprise. Surprise over property.

EIGHT OF DIAMONDS (inheritance) you will inherit something, like a home or furnishings for the home; or you will buy a home and it is financed through small payments—or a home is sold with small payments.

SEVEN OF DIAMONDS (success) your success started through your early training at home; or you will have a successful home or will succeed as a homemaker or builder; or success in selling or buying a home.

Club Suit

ACE OF CLUBS (gift) you will receive a gift for the home—new furniture, musical instruments, or some large object; or you will receive the deed to a new home.

KING OF CLUBS (vocation) you will have business transactions in the home; or your business will be connected with the home in some way; or your goal is working for a new home.

QUEEN OF CLUBS (inquirer) a new home is coming to you and your home will be run like a business and afford much comfort.

JACK OF CLUBS (relatives) relatives will live with you; or you will live with them; or very close friends or relatives influence your home conditions.

TEN OF CLUBS (journey) your next move will be a better home; or the sale of the place you live in. A change comes into the home or home conditions. You may buy a country home.

NINE OF CLUBS (luck) through luck you will sometime in your life obtain a home to your liking. This home may come through a gamble of some kind, such as playing the stock exchange, etc.; or you will have good luck if you buy a home of your own. Luck and a home go together here.

EIGHT OF CLUBS (achievement) home conditions or someone where you live will help you with some achievement or business. If a contractor, good business for you.

SEVEN OF CLUBS (messages) a message of some kind comes to you about someone who is going to call; also indicates you like apartment or hotel life. If a contractor, many calls for construction work.

Spade Suit

ACE OF SPADES (death) there has been or will be sickness or death in your home or immediate surroundings; or in the neighborhood; or old neighbors move away; or relatives move.

KING OF SPADES (callers) a caller will come and take you to someone very ill; or an ambulance calls near you; or the police call for information regarding an accident you have seen or will see; a disagreeable caller; or a caller to repair something in the home—a plumber, etc.

QUEEN OF SPADES (gratitude) an ungrateful person calls at your home; or an ungrateful person works for you.

JACK OF SPADES (compass-thoughts) someone sends evil thoughts into your home; or a robber may enter your home. Lock your doors and windows when you leave the house. Also indicates a depressing condition in the home. Relax and be happy.

TEN OF SPADES (sun) you should be careful of fire where you live and some damage caused by fire; or you will install new electric fixtures or outlets in your house.

NINE OF SPADES (disappointment) a loss of home or something where you live; indicates the need of something new in the home and a delay in getting it; or dissatisfaction where you live; or an old miserable condition is ended; or buying a new home.

EIGHT OF SPADES (trouble) you should be careful of a fall where you live; indicates a dissatisfied condition where you live; or trouble at home; or worry over some home condition; or trouble with landlord or ungrateful tenants. Concentrate and clear this up.

SEVEN OF SPADES (health) a home condition affects your health; or you are sick at heart because you can't afford something for the home; or you want to move; or someone moves away and you shed tears.

House of Journey

Heart Suit

ACE OF HEARTS (the abode) in the House of Journey indicates a change of abode; or the change of furniture or something pertaining to where you live; or someone moves from your home.

KING OF HEARTS (enjoyment) a kindly person will come from a trip to visit you, and you will enjoy their company and have many nice times together.

QUEEN OF HEARTS (friends) some friends will call to visit you after a trip. Look for guests.

JACK OF HEARTS (popularity) by being popular and well liked you will be invited on a pleasure trip. If a pilot, train engineer, or bus driver, you will be steadily employed.

TEN OF HEARTS (marriage or union) some newlyweds will call on you; or some friends or relatives from a distance will hold a reunion and you will enjoy yourself. If single, when married a honeymoon trip.

NINE OF HEARTS (your wish) a change of some kind has something to do with your wish—possibly a trip; or a big change comes into your life—a move.

EIGHT OF HEARTS (moon-love) you will love a trip you are going to make. If single, you may meet someone you will love. A change for the better.

SEVEN OF HEARTS (happiness) a change of something to your benefit that will make you happy. This change eliminates a lot of jealousy. A shopping trip soon.

> ... *of journeying the benefits are many; the freshness it bringeth to the heart, the seeing and hearing of marvelous things; the delight of beholding new cities, the meeting of unknown friends, the learning of high manners*
>
> —Sandi the Gulistan

Diamond Suit

ACE OF DIAMONDS (new undertaking) you may change the work you are doing; or you are going into a new venture of some kind that should be successful; or you will change location or job or business.

KING OF DIAMONDS (legal papers) you may have to take a trip due to some legal procedure; or some papers will be sent to you from a distance; or some sort of papers from a distance will bring you news or knowledge you want—something you will read or sign.

QUEEN OF DIAMONDS (seasons) before this month has passed you will take a trip or make a change of some kind; should better financial conditions.

JACK OF DIAMONDS (letters) an important paper or hasty news about a change is coming soon from a long distance.

TEN OF DIAMONDS (money) you will receive money from a journey; or by taking a journey you will get some. Money is connected with a change or trip here. If you travel—good business.

NINE OF DIAMONDS (surprises) you will be surprised about a trip of some kind; either someone calls from a distance or you will be invited on a trip; or you will be surprised about a change of plans.

EIGHT OF DIAMONDS (inheritance) money will come to you from a distance; or in order to claim an inheritance, you will have to make a trip. If in business, money is sent from many places.

SEVEN OF DIAMONDS (success) through a change of conditions or a trip, you will bring about success; or if you are contemplating a trip, it will be successful and free from danger.

Club Suit

ACE OF CLUBS (gift) a present of some kind is connected with a trip; it could be a new car or the money to take a trip; or a proposition made to change your position or business location.

KING OF CLUBS (vocation) if a traveling person, you can expect plenty of work; or your next vocation will involve travel in some way, or any line connected with transportation. You should find this a successful vocation; a business trip.

QUEEN OF CLUBS (inquirer) you are facing a journey, a move, or a change of some kind.

JACK OF CLUBS (relatives) you will receive a message or word from a relative; or a letter from someone who is traveling; or relatives or friends will come to you.

TEN OF CLUBS (journey) in your lifetime a big change is coming; you may move far away from where you were born; or you may take a long sea voyage; a long trip by automobile, train, or plane.

NINE OF CLUBS (luck) if you are contemplating a change or trip, this will be to your advantage as it will bring you good luck.

EIGHT OF CLUBS (achievement) through some achievement, your own or someone else's, the conditions in your life will change. This change comes through the source of your support. If in business—good business.

SEVEN OF CLUBS (messages) a message comes causing you to make a trip or asking you on a trip; or telling you someone is coming on a trip; could be a long-distance phone call.

He who never leaves his country is full of prejudices.

—Carlo Goldini

Spade Suit

ACE OF SPADES (death) you will take a trip because of a death; or you hear of a death some distance from you; or a hurried trip on account of a death; or you will go to a funeral.

KING OF SPADES (callers) someone calls to tell you about a death; or police call bringing bad news concerning an accident to someone you know; or you get a speeding ticket while driving; or uninvited guests arrive.

QUEEN OF SPADES (gratitude) someone will be ungrateful for a trip you have taken or will take them on; or you will go with friends on a trip and return disgusted; or you will be grateful for a change of condition that takes place.

JACK OF SPADES (compass-thoughts) you may meet a very deceitful person on a trip. Beware of the people you meet. If professional person, you will travel by plane to theatres for appearances.

TEN OF SPADES (sun) through a trip you will investigate something you want to know; also indicates a short trip somewhere in the late afternoon or evening; or the sun will shine for you in making a change.

NINE OF SPADES (disappointment) you will be disappointed in a trip or in not taking a trip you planned; or a big loss through a trip or change of some kind is imminent; or a delay in plans—to move or sell.

EIGHT OF SPADES (trouble) there is trouble regarding a journey. Don't take a trip this week if you are planning one; consult *Gong Hee Fot Choy* next week and see how the cards run then.

SEVEN OF SPADES (health) you will take a trip to visit a sick friend; or you will take a trip for your health; or a new baby in the family; or worry over a change (never worry).

House of Papers

Heart Suit

ACE OF HEARTS (the abode) in the House of Papers indicates that you will sign a lease or mortgage or some kind of paper involving the home. It could be only a rent receipt or buying or selling a house.

KING OF HEARTS (enjoyment) some stocks or bonds or insurance papers will be given to you or placed so you may finance them easily through a dear friend or relative.

QUEEN OF HEARTS (friends) you will sign a paper a friend brings to you, like a will.

JACK OF HEARTS (popularity) through being popular, you may win something where papers are signed; or you will sign a note for a friend, or for a purchase you make. If in movies, you sign a contract.

TEN OF HEARTS (marriage or union) you will sign a wedding certificate, yours or a friend's; or you will sign as a witness to something—a business contract, or the amalgamation of firms.

NINE OF HEARTS (your wish) if your wish has paper involved, you should get your wish.

EIGHT OF HEARTS (moon-love) someone loves you and will make their will or insurance in your favor.

SEVEN OF HEARTS (happiness) you will receive some paper pertaining to finance that will make you very happy; also, might be graduation papers or a diploma; or a wedding license—a paper of importance.

The moving finger writes;
And having writ,
Moves on; nor all the Piety nor wit
Shall lure it back to cancel half a line,
Nor all the tears wash out a word of it.

—Rubaiyat of Omar Khayyam

Diamond Suit

ACE OF DIAMONDS (new undertaking) in a new undertaking have all papers drawn up carefully; also indicates that you will sign a legal document and benefit by it.

KING OF DIAMONDS (legal papers) any lawsuit you have or any legal papers you sign will be in your favor this coming year. There is something pertaining to papers here for you.

QUEEN OF DIAMONDS (seasons) you may be called into court, either as a witness, jury duty, or to protect your own interests. Something where time is set for your appearance; or a business deal closed.

JACK OF DIAMONDS (letters) you will receive a legal document through the mail or a telegram about court action; or you will follow in the newspapers some trial that takes place. Hasty air news of importance.

TEN OF DIAMONDS (money) through a legal action you will receive money; in some way you must sign a paper. Use care in what you sign, and avoid going to court later. Money through signing a paper.

NINE OF DIAMONDS (surprises) you will be surprised by a subpoena or court action of some kind where you will be involved; or someone will want you to sign a paper; or a surprise over a position offered if a secretary. (Be careful.)

EIGHT OF DIAMONDS (inheritance) you will have to go into court over an inheritance, or sign papers with the help of an attorney. If a secretary, you will work for a doctor or lawyer.

SEVEN OF DIAMONDS (success) your success comes through some court or legal matter where papers are involved; or successful work where papers are handled; also you will sign a paper, either a will or a lease.

Club Suit

ACE OF CLUBS (gift) the gift of stocks or bonds or shares in a business; something in which paper plays an important part; or a gift of paper will be recorded.

KING OF CLUBS (vocation) your vocation should be where papers are signed or handled; or through the newspaper you find a position; papers have something to do with your work or future support.

QUEEN OF CLUBS (inquirer) papers of a legal type will be signed by you; perhaps you know about these papers now; or papers signed for something you bought or sold.

JACK OF CLUBS (relatives) you will be involved with relatives, very close business associates, or friends in court; or you will go or be called to court as a witness.

TEN OF CLUBS (journey) papers of some kind bring a change in your life, such as selling a home, land, or property of some kind; or you will have to take a trip to settle some legal action or sell some property; or a changed contract.

NINE OF CLUBS (luck) a lucky investment or a paper of some kind will affect your future; also indicates luck in a legal action; something pertaining to court.

EIGHT OF CLUBS (achievement) papers and business come together here; you buy or sell a business, or something where you make a profit. This also concerns the source of your support. Good business.

SEVEN OF CLUBS (messages) you will receive a message about a paper of some kind; or you sign for a package you receive; or a telephone conversation regarding a contract or signing of a paper.

Discourage litigation; persuade your neighbors
to compromise whenever you can.

—Abraham Lincoln

Spade Suit

ACE OF SPADES (death) you will read in the newspapers about the death of a friend or prominent person; or you will sign a paper regarding the death of someone; or care for papers of a deceased person; or take care of papers for an absent person.

KING OF SPADES (callers) callers will interest you with something they saw in the newspapers; or a caller whom you dislike comes; or someone wants you to sign a note; or a caller asks you to sign for a purchase. This caller is a person you would rather not see.

QUEEN OF SPADES (gratitude) an ungrateful person will try to gain something through you—like being named in your will or made beneficiary in insurance papers; or you will be grateful to someone for helping you with your lesson or signing a paper.

JACK OF SPADES (compass-thoughts) you will have a legal tilt over insurance papers; or someone may try to cheat you out of what is rightfully yours in some paper. Be careful. Or news you are waiting for comes over the air.

TEN OF SPADES (sun) you may sign a marriage license as a witness; or find a paper that has long been missing. Put papers in a safe place. The sun will shine for you when you sign a certain paper.

NINE OF SPADES (disappointment) you will lose a valuable paper; or you will sign a paper incorrectly and thereby lose much; or a delay will occur in consummating a contract. An attorney should help you sign important papers.

EIGHT OF SPADES (trouble) you will have trouble over a class paper if attending school—you may fail in an examination; or you will have trouble over signing a paper; or you misplace a valuable paper.

SEVEN OF SPADES (health) something in the newspaper will make you heartsick; or someone's illness makes you blue; or you may sign a will as witness; or you will visit a dentist or doctor—cheer up.

House of Vocation

Heart Suit

ACE OF HEARTS (the abode) in the House of Vocation indicates that some occupation that could be done in the home would be to your benefit; or you love housework.

KING OF HEARTS (enjoyment) you should cultivate a cheerful disposition which will help you, or happiness in your work, or your work will be for or with very nice people; or you enjoy your work.

QUEEN OF HEARTS (friends) you will make many friends where you work, or a friend will give you work if unemployed; or through an agency you will secure a good position.

JACK OF HEARTS (popularity) you should be popular where you are employed; or your work will be with something very popular. Could be with the film industry.

TEN OF HEARTS (marriage or union) through the union of some business you will be employed if out of work; or, if working, a raise in pay. If single, through marriage you will change your work; or you will be taken into the firm you work for.

NINE OF HEARTS (your wish) if you have wished for work you will soon be employed; or get something better in your line of endeavor. You should get your wish.

EIGHT OF HEARTS (moon-love) if you are working you should love the work you are doing; or if you get a new position, you will like the work very much.

SEVEN OF HEARTS (happiness) you will either be happy over a proposition offered or a new job or position, or a raise in salary; or a better change of positions.

> Don't worry and fret, faint-hearted
> The chances have just begun,
> For the best jobs haven't been started,
> The best work hasn't been done.
>
> —Berton Braley

Diamond Suit

ACE OF DIAMONDS (new undertaking) you should start a new under-taking; something new is in store for you in your line of endeavor. A new start for you is here.

KING OF DIAMONDS (legal papers) you would be good in the military or a teacher, judge, head of an organization or any position where leadership is required; you will be employed by a prosperous person.

QUEEN OF DIAMONDS (seasons) you should prosper in work requiring patience and time. Also if unemployed, you will receive a position or the equivalent soon; or you will change your employment.

JACK OF DIAMONDS (letters) you will make good where speed is needed in handling things—speed of mind or action; or where things must be carried out with accuracy; or you may work with the communi-cations industry.

TEN OF DIAMONDS (money) your present or future vocation will bring you much money; also indicates banking business or a deal in stocks and bonds or securities—where money comes through handling of papers, or money is received in paper.

NINE OF DIAMONDS (surprises) you will be surprised about your work and something better is in store for you; if unemployed, you will secure employment without your efforts, or will receive a surprise about an offer made.

EIGHT OF DIAMONDS (inheritance) sometime in your life you will take another person's job due to death; or you will inherit some business or business shares, or constant income.

SEVEN OF DIAMONDS (success) a very successful future; or you will go into something that brings success; or you plunge into something your-self; successful employment.

Club Suit

ACE OF CLUBS (gift) you should be a gifted person, and success is in store for you if you apply this gift rightly. If employed, you will sell small articles.

KING OF CLUBS (vocation) a new vocation is in store for you, and you should succeed. If unemployed, you will be employed soon; or you are a tireless, good worker and plenty of work is in store for you.

QUEEN OF CLUBS (inquirer) work is in store for you; or you like to work; or you will take up a new line of endeavor. Work and business indicated.

JACK OF CLUBS (relatives) your vocation is connected with your relatives; you either will work for them, or will work at or do something to please them.

TEN OF CLUBS (journey) your vocation will have something to do with travel; or you will change it many times during your life; or you will work at the same thing in many places or jobs; or you will travel a distance to your work. Your future work will involve space and distance.

NINE OF CLUBS (luck) you will be lucky in whatever you do, bringing good things into your life. Luck and work.

EIGHT OF CLUBS (achievement) you will achieve great things in the business world, a bright future in whatever you are doing or are going to do; good work or business is coming.

SEVEN OF CLUBS (messages) someone will call to offer you work; or talk over business with you. A message concerning something you are doing or studying.

> *Each man has his own vocation*
> *The talent is the call.*

—Ralph Waldo Emerson

Spade Suit

ACE OF SPADES (death) in your lifetime you will want to follow a dangerous vocation like flying, racing fast cars, testing explosives or chemicals, working on high tension wires, or anything dangerous. Use care in your work.

KING OF SPADES (callers) someone will tell you to follow his line of work; or a caller seeks your services. Don't let yourself be influenced.

QUEEN OF SPADES (gratitude) you have been hindered in what you are doing through nagging relatives; or hampered through money; or people do not appreciate your loyal service or what you do for them.

JACK OF SPADES (compass-thoughts) just thinking of what you like to do will never get you anywhere. Concentrate on what you want to do, then do it. Grasp opportunities, or you lose out. Unlooked-for opportunity.

TEN OF SPADES (sun) you should be sure your vocation is an honorable one, or that you do not work for a schemer or crook. You might be involved. You will uncover something crooked. If a gardener, plenty of work in store. If a laborer, you will be steadily employed where bright lights are made or used.

NINE OF SPADES (disappointment) you are disappointed in the outcome of some work; or are disappointed in not being employed; a loss of employment indicated here; or a delay in completing a job.

EIGHT OF SPADES (trouble) if unemployed, you will have trouble finding work; or you will have to overcome great obstacles in your work. Strive hard—you will win.

SEVEN OF SPADES (health) your health or another's will play an important part in your work; you may be deterred by having to care for a sick or disabled person. If a doctor or nurse, you will have many patients.

House of Marriage

Heart Suit

ACE OF HEARTS (the abode) if single, you may soon get married and have a new abode. If married, either a move, a new home, or someone comes to live with you.

KING OF HEARTS (enjoyment) if married, your life should be happy; if single, a nice person will ask you to get married.

QUEEN OF HEARTS (friends) a friend of yours will soon be married, someone very close to you, like an aunt.

JACK OF HEARTS (popularity) a very popular person you know will be married soon, and you will attend the wedding.

TEN OF HEARTS (marriage or union) if you are single, you sure as fate will be married soon; or if you have children old enough to marry, one will get married; or a marriage takes place for someone close to you; or a reunion of old friends or relatives.

NINE OF HEARTS (your wish) if you wished about getting married or for the return of someone, you will get your wish.

EIGHT OF HEARTS (moon-love) if single, love and marriage will soon come into your life; if married, your mate loves you.

SEVEN OF HEARTS (happiness) you will attend a wedding and you will enjoy the good time.

> *Therefore shall a man leave his father and his mother, and shall cleave unto his wife; and they shall be one flesh.*

—Genesis II, 24

Diamond Suit

ACE OF DIAMONDS (new undertaking) through being successful in a new undertaking, you will marry; a marriage will come as a new undertaking; or you will unite with others in a new venture.

KING OF DIAMONDS (legal papers) you will sign a wedding certificate, your own or another's. If married, you may have to sign a paper regarding your mate's affairs, where an attorney is present.

QUEEN OF DIAMONDS (seasons) if you are not married before the season is past, you will have an offer of marriage soon; or you will attend the wedding of a friend.

JACK OF DIAMONDS (letters) you will receive news of a wedding or from newlyweds; or news of an elopement.

TEN OF DIAMONDS (money) through marriage you will obtain money; your mate will be successful with your help; or a mercenary marriage, or a wealthy marriage.

NINE OF DIAMONDS (surprises) you will be surprised about an old person's wedding; or when you hear of the marriage of someone whom you thought never would wed; or some proposal will surprise you.

EIGHT OF DIAMONDS (inheritance) you attend a marriage; or the union with old folks, like taking care of them; you will inherit some money; or jewelry or personal belongings.

SEVEN OF DIAMONDS (success) if married, your life should be successful; also, your mate should be kind and true.

Club Suit

ACE OF CLUBS (gift) you will give a wedding present or receive one; or a gift for the family.

KING OF CLUBS (vocation) if you are single, your new vocation will be keeping house; or through a marriage or union of some business, you will change your vocation; or you will get a position with newlyweds; or someone gets married and you get their position.

QUEEN OF CLUBS (inquirer) if you are single, you will be married soon; or a marriage comes to your family or where you are living; you will have something to do with the marriage; or the union of something.

JACK OF CLUBS (relatives) a relative or friend of yours will be married soon; a young person or a relative will visit you; or a birth.

TEN OF CLUBS (journey) a honeymoon if single; or a trip with your sweetheart; or a trip that will reunite you with a loved one; or the union of relatives or friends.

NINE OF CLUBS (luck) your marriage will prove lucky, and your mate will supply you with many worldly goods; or if single, you will be married soon.

EIGHT OF CLUBS (achievement) your marriage depends on something you are doing; or you will achieve something through your mate; or a marriage for business reasons only; or the union of business by marriage.

SEVEN OF CLUBS (messages) you will receive a message to attend a wedding; or hear of an elopement or marriage. If a businessperson, you may hear of some firms merging, which will benefit your own business.

Spade Suit

ACE OF SPADES (death) a death separates you from someone with whom you are united—like marriage, relatives, or a friendship of long standing; or divorce or uncontrolled separation from loved ones.

KING OF SPADES (callers) a relative or friend who calls will try to break up your home; or callers will tell of their wedding plans; or by associating with certain people, you may be arrested. Be careful of the friends you make.

QUEEN OF SPADES (gratitude) if married, you can expect ingratitude from your in-laws; or from people closely associated with you; or your family is very grateful.

JACK OF SPADES (compass-thoughts) a conniving, cunning person may try to break up your romance or marriage. Watch for this party; may be a new acquaintance. Trickery of some kind.

TEN OF SPADES (sun) the sun will not shine every day in marriage; also indicates you will discover something about an associate that causes you to reprimand him.

NINE OF SPADES (disappointment) you will be disappointed in a marriage or you have lost someone in your home through marriage; or you will be divorced; or a mate is taken by death. A disappointment connected with marriage; or a delay in wedding plans.

EIGHT OF SPADES (trouble) you will have trouble in your marriage over money or relatives; or you will be a peacemaker between married persons; or you will have a falling out with friends; or you wish guests would leave.

SEVEN OF SPADES (health) your health or another's will affect your marriage; or you are blue after your marriage—not necessarily about your mate but maybe financial trouble. Cheer up—good days ahead.

House of Happiness

Heart Suit

ACE OF HEARTS (the abode) in the House of Happiness indicates that happiness should come through a good home and thrifty mate.

KING OF HEARTS (enjoyment) happiness comes through kindness and love; also, sweetheart, wife, husband, or children.

QUEEN OF HEARTS (friends) happiness comes through good friends; or you are a favorite of an aunt. If single, admiration from a lovely boy or girl.

JACK OF HEARTS (popularity) happiness is in store by being popular with your friends and business associates. If young and aspiring to theatrical work, fame will bring happiness in the future.

TEN OF HEARTS (marriage or union) you will be very happy about some marriage that will take place, either your own if single, or a very close friend or relative. A happy union or marriage.

NINE OF HEARTS (your wish) your wish could bring much happiness if you get it. You should get your wish.

EIGHT OF HEARTS (moon-love) your happiness lies in the respect and love bestowed upon you by others. If single, happiness over a proposal.

SEVEN OF HEARTS (happiness) you can be sure for a long time to come that happiness is in store for you. Don't let jealousy on your part spoil this happiness. If single, may be an engagement ring soon.

> *Happiness in this world, when it comes, comes incidentally, make it the object of pursuit, and it leads us a wild-goose chase, and is never attained.*

—Nathaniel Hawthorne, *Journals* 21 Oct., 1852

Diamond Suit

ACE OF DIAMONDS (new undertaking) something you are doing or are about to do will bring you happiness; also, you will find happiness in doing for others.

KING OF DIAMONDS (legal papers) something in a legal form will influence your happiness; also happiness through relatives or friends. If single, you will associate with professional people.

QUEEN OF DIAMONDS (seasons) you are very unhappy when you have to wait for an appointment; also indicates that time affects your future happiness.

JACK OF DIAMONDS (letters) you will receive hasty news that brings you happiness. Love letter or an invitation.

TEN OF DIAMONDS (money) happiness will come through some achievement that brings money; also when saving for a rainy day.

NINE OF DIAMONDS (surprises) a surprise you receive within a week will bring you happiness.

EIGHT OF DIAMONDS (inheritance) an inheritance you receive will make you happy; also happiness comes from a loving home and a thrifty mate. Steady income.

SEVEN OF DIAMONDS (success) success and happiness are in store for you; also, you should be very happy with business associates and when traveling.

Club Suit

ACE OF CLUBS (gift) a gift you receive will make you very happy; this will be something very nice.

KING OF CLUBS (vocation) by being employed, you will be very happy; or your happiness comes through your work. Happiness comes with a vocation.

QUEEN OF CLUBS (inquirer) much happiness is in store for you.

JACK OF CLUBS (relatives) relatives influence your happiness; if they interfere, like a mother-in-law or some other interfering person, get away from their influence.

TEN OF CLUBS (journey) your greatest happiness comes through travel. See the world if you can. A stone gathers no moss while rolling, but it gains a high polish. Happiness comes over change of conditions—a good change, could be buying or selling property.

NINE OF CLUBS (luck) some good fortune you have soon will make you very jubilant and happy.

EIGHT OF CLUBS (achievement) you should be very happy where you work or with some achievement of yours; or by good business.

SEVEN OF CLUBS (messages) you will receive many kinds of invitations that make you happy; or a message from someone who pleases you.

We deem those happy who, from the experience of life, have learned to bear ills, without being overcome by them.

—Juvenal

Spade Suit

ACE OF SPADES (death) happiness will come into your life through the death of someone near you who has been suffering for a long time; or you will be very unhappy because of the death of someone you love. Tears are indicated. The elimination of an angry person or condition will bring happiness.

KING OF SPADES (callers) callers will tell of someone being put in jail or arrested; or something stolen is recovered. Indicates justice in some wrong deed. Or someone calls you are happy to see.

QUEEN OF SPADES (gratitude) a grateful person will express his happiness for a favor bestowed by someone.

JACK OF SPADES (compass-thoughts) an agent will try to sell you something you don't want; or a suitor whom you dislike calls; or you will be disgusted with poor radio or TV programs.

TEN OF SPADES (sun) people will call to find out something they wish to know, like prying into your business. Beware of a gossip. Or the sun will shine through a caller you have not seen in a long time.

NINE OF SPADES (disappointment) someone you expect to call or dine with will not arrive; a delayed business conference; something unexpected happens; you will hear about it and will feel badly.

EIGHT OF SPADES (trouble) you are very unhappy when you are not in your own line of endeavor; or you will have trouble with someone who calls. Something disagreeable connected with a caller. Angry words.

SEVEN OF SPADES (health) good health will bring you happiness; also, you are very unhappy if poorly dressed—makes you feel sick all over. Get new clothes if needed—they give you a lift.

House of Enjoyment

Heart Suit

ACE OF HEARTS (the abode) in the House of Enjoyment indicates that you will enjoy a party where you live or will have an invitation to someone's home. Also indicates you enjoy a good home.

KING OF HEARTS (enjoyment) enjoyment and happiness come through being entertained by someone who loves you; or being in the company of a certain person. This is a sure sign that happiness is in store for you.

QUEEN OF HEARTS (friends) enjoyment comes from many invitations from loving friends; and you enjoy your friends' company. An aunt has your best interest at heart.

JACK OF HEARTS (popularity) you enjoy popularity and enjoy being in the company of noted people. If young, you will enjoy fame.

TEN OF HEARTS (marriage or union) you get great enjoyment at weddings and entertaining friends. You should love company.

NINE OF HEARTS (your wish) if you wished about something that brings enjoyment, you should get your wish; also you love beautiful clothes.

EIGHT OF HEARTS (moon-love) if you are single, you will have the love of someone whose company you enjoy very much. If married, your friends love you and enjoy your company.

SEVEN OF HEARTS (happiness) many nice invitations will come to you within the month that you should enjoy immensely; some new clothing is enjoyed by you.

It's pretty hard to tell what does bring enjoyment.
Poverty an' wealth have both failed.

—Kin Hubbard

Diamond Suit

ACE OF DIAMONDS (new undertaking) you will enjoy something you have accomplished; also indicates an invitation to a card party or lodge affair; or you may go into business where people come to enjoy themselves.

KING OF DIAMONDS (legal papers) you will receive an invitation to a party where an engagement is announced—a bridal or layette shower. Also you may receive a gift on paper that will need recording.

QUEEN OF DIAMONDS (seasons) in time you will be connected with a charitable organization, where you will give entertainments and dinners to raise money for a good cause; or soon you will attend such a dinner.

JACK OF DIAMONDS (letters) you will receive an invitation to a dance, a wedding, or a theatre party; you will enjoy yourself immensely.

TEN OF DIAMONDS (money) soon the receipt of money will give you great enjoyment; also you will have many invitations from wealthy friends.

NINE OF DIAMONDS (surprises) a surprise party is given in your honor; or you may go on an outing, go horseback riding, swimming, hiking, or on a picnic—an enjoyable surprise.

EIGHT OF DIAMONDS (inheritance) something you will enjoy very much will be given you, like jewelry or something you want badly—maybe an inheritance.

SEVEN OF DIAMONDS (success) your own success or someone else's gives you enjoyment; an introduction at a weekend party will bring you success later; or success through entertainment.

Club Suit

ACE OF CLUBS (gift) you will enjoy a gift you receive and share with others, like a new car or TV; something others can share.

KING OF CLUBS (vocation) you enjoy whatever you do; also you will be required to help with some sort of entertainment—this includes anything from being a member of a banquet committee to actually playing a part in the entertainment.

QUEEN OF CLUBS (inquirer) good times are in store for you; many invitations; visitors and callers.

JACK OF CLUBS (relatives) relatives will bring enjoyment into your life. Enjoyment comes through children or good friends.

TEN OF CLUBS (journey) you are going on a shopping trip, and you will enjoy the things you purchase; or get good bargains; or you will enjoy a trip.

NINE OF CLUBS (luck) some good luck brings you enjoyment; you will meet nice friends who will entertain you.

EIGHT OF CLUBS (achievement) good luck in work or business; or something is placed in your way to help you; something will give you great enjoyment.

SEVEN OF CLUBS (messages) you will receive many messages or phone calls and invitations that will bring you enjoyment.

> *Man could direct his ways by plain reason, and support his life by tasteless food; but God has given us wit and flavour, and brightness, and laughter, and perfumes, to enliven the days of man's pilgrimage, and to "charm his painted steps over the burning marble."*
>
> —Sidney Smith

Spade Suit

ACE OF SPADES (death) you will enjoy the termination of something personal, like a contract paid in full; or the end of a burden of some kind.

KING OF SPADES (callers) callers will annoy you; such as an intoxicated person coming to your house; or you will attend a party where someone is so intoxicated that the police are called; or you will enjoy a call from an old friend.

QUEEN OF SPADES (gratitude) by being grateful for small favors, much happiness comes into your life; cultivate a grateful manner.

JACK OF SPADES (compass-thoughts) someone is thinking of you and planning to take you where you will enjoy yourself; beware of someone who could cause you unhappiness through flattery. You may visit a radio or TV station.

TEN OF SPADES (sun) outdoor sports should bring you happiness; or you enjoy the sunshine and fresh air.

NINE OF SPADES (disappointment) some place you go will disappoint you, like at a dinner the food is poor, or at a dance the music is not to your liking; or you may lose something at a place of amusement and feel badly about it; or a postponement of a date.

EIGHT OF SPADES (trouble) if you go out to have a good time, you have car trouble, or your escort insults you (take mad money or roller skates), or you have trouble later with someone for going.

SEVEN OF SPADES (health) you should enjoy health for years to come; take care of it. If ill, you will have a speedy recovery; or your enjoyment is spoiled by poor health. Cheer up—time changes everything.

House of Messages

Heart Suit

ACE OF HEARTS (the abode) in the House of Messages indicates that you will receive a message about something pertaining to where you live or about something you bought for the home.

KING OF HEARTS (enjoyment) you will receive a message from someone asking you to a dinner party. Also a message from an attorney or doctor—important message.

QUEEN OF HEARTS (friends) a message from friends telling you about some good time they are going to have and they will ask you to join them. A pleasant message; a shopping trip.

JACK OF HEARTS (popularity) you will receive an invitation to go some place because you are popular; or you will be in the company of some very noted person.

TEN OF HEARTS (marriage or union) you will receive a message concerning an elopement or marriage.

NINE OF HEARTS (your wish) if you wished to hear from someone soon, you will get your wish. Also you will receive a message concerning your wish.

EIGHT OF HEARTS (moon-love) you will receive a message from someone who loves you. A love message.

SEVEN OF HEARTS (happiness) an unexpected message will come to you that brings happiness with it. Something good.

> Kind messages, that pass from land to land;
> Kind letters, that betray the heart's deep history,
> In which we feel the pressure of a hand—
> One touch of fire—and all the rest is mystery.

—Henry Wadsworth Longfellow

Diamond Suit

ACE OF DIAMONDS (new undertaking) you will receive a message offering a new job, position, or business proposition.

KING OF DIAMONDS (legal papers) if you are a writer, you will receive a telephone call regarding some article, play, etc.; an artist, a call about art; a layman, a call about an investment. Information about something that is used in everyday life and where a paper could be involved.

QUEEN OF DIAMONDS (seasons) a telephone call or message will be received, setting the time for something you are to do, or meet someone.

JACK OF DIAMONDS (letters) a messenger or mailman will call, bringing hasty news about investments or business; hasty news of some sort.

TEN OF DIAMONDS (money) you will receive a message or talk over the phone about money; arrange payments on something you bought or money you will receive. It's a message concerning money.

NINE OF DIAMONDS (surprises) you will receive a message containing a surprise; a good surprise.

EIGHT OF DIAMONDS (inheritance) you will receive a message about an inheritance; or an opportunity to invest money that should bring good returns.

SEVEN OF DIAMONDS (success) you will receive an important message which influences your future success. Concentrate here when this comes your way. Important.

Club Suit

ACE OF CLUBS (gift) a message about a gift comes with a ring of the bell; or a telephone call; or the delivery of a gift; or a proposition offered over the phone.

KING OF CLUBS (vocation) if you are unemployed, someone will send money or phone you asking for your services; or a message comes regarding your advice in a matter.

QUEEN OF CLUBS (inquirer) a message comes from a distance to you; or you will receive mail advertising a trip or inviting you on one.

JACK OF CLUBS (relatives) a relative will phone you about a scandal or write about it; or an invitation to one of their weddings.

TEN OF CLUBS (journey) a message comes from a distance to you; or you will receive mail advertising a trip or inviting you on one.

NINE OF CLUBS (luck) a message or tip from someone on a race or a chance in gambling will prove lucky to you; a lucky message of some kind.

EIGHT OF CLUBS (achievement) a message you receive will have something to do with your achievement; or a message about business helps you. Don't quit school to work. Business talk by phone.

SEVEN OF CLUBS (messages) if you are expecting a message regarding your wish, you will surely get it and it will be advantageous. If working, your employment should be where many phone calls are received.

> *He whistles as he goes, light-hearted wretch, cold and yet cheerful; messenger of grief perhaps to thousands, and of joy to some.*

—James Fenimore Cooper

Spade Suit

ACE OF SPADES (death) you will receive a message concerning a death; or an accident and a death follows; or someone will call to say goodbye.

KING OF SPADES (callers) you should be careful of what you write in a message or say in a telephone conversation; also might mean an order canceled, if in business; or someone phones they are going to visit.

QUEEN OF SPADES (gratitude) you will hear gossip over the phone or in a letter; or you will receive a mean letter from an ungrateful person; or you will be grateful to hear from someone.

JACK OF SPADES (compass-thoughts) if you suspect a person, investigate. This person doesn't even like himself. Deceit is evident. A deceitful borrower; or you will hear unpleasant news broadcast.

TEN OF SPADES (sun) you will receive a beneficial message this afternoon or early in the evening regarding business or personal affairs; something you are wanting to know.

NINE OF SPADES (disappointment) you will receive a message relating a loss of some kind; or you will lose something and send a message or phone trying to locate it; or a delayed phone call.

EIGHT OF SPADES (trouble) you will receive a message relating a trouble of some kind; or you will lose something and send a message or phone trying to locate it; or a delayed phone call.

SEVEN OF SPADES (health) you will hear of the illness of someone you thought in good health; or you hear something that makes you blue and sick at heart; or a message inquiring about your health.

House of Relatives

Heart Suit

ACE OF HEARTS (the abode) in the House of Relatives indicates that relatives will influence your home; or will help you get a home; or you will live with them or they with you; or friends or relatives will visit you.

KING OF HEARTS (enjoyment) a kindly person, like a father, an uncle, or some relative will be good to you; also financial gains through this party.

QUEEN OF HEARTS (friends) you will have many friends where you live, and they will be as dear as relatives.

JACK OF HEARTS (popularity) there should be someone in your immediate family who is famous, and this party should be kind to you. Also, if married and have children, one will be very popular as time goes on. If married, your mate may become famous.

TEN OF HEARTS (marriage or union) one of your relatives will be married soon; or you will attend the wedding of a close friend; or you attend a reunion of your relatives soon.

NINE OF HEARTS (your wish) a relatives influences your wish. Also this could be a close friend; sometimes friends are as dear as relatives. You should get your wish.

EIGHT OF HEARTS (moon-love) some or one of your relatives loves you very much and you are the favorite. If you have children, natural or adopted, they will bestow much love on you. As a whole, friends and relatives love you.

SEVEN OF HEARTS (happiness) you should derive much happiness through your relatives; also there is a little jealousy from some of them.

> We are given our relatives but we should be
> Thankful that we can choose our friends.
>
> —Addison Mizner

Diamond Suit

ACE OF DIAMONDS (new undertaking) you and a relative or very close friend will start a new undertaking; caution is needed here. Be sure you handle this in a business way, as with a stranger.

KING OF DIAMONDS (legal papers) you may sign a paper with a relative. Handle this matter in a legal way. Misunderstanding in family; or your family will need an attorney's services soon; or you have a professional person in your family.

QUEEN OF DIAMONDS (seasons) if you have children, a child will become very prominent in the world. Time brings more relatives into your life that will be a blessing in years to come.

JACK OF DIAMONDS (letters) you will receive from a relative hasty news that is very important to you.

TEN OF DIAMONDS (money) you should receive money from a person closely related to you.

NINE OF DIAMONDS (surprises) a relative will surprise you; something they do or say will surprise you.

EIGHT OF DIAMONDS (inheritance) you may inherit stocks, bonds, or furniture from a relative at a later date, you are their favorite; or small sums of money given.

SEVEN OF DIAMONDS (success) your success lies through a relative. Follow their advice as it is good for you. Successful friends or relatives.

Club Suit

ACE OF CLUBS (gift) you will receive a gift from a relative; or from a close friend; or a new baby may join the family circle; a birth.

KING OF CLUBS (vocation) you will either work with or for relatives; they will have something to do with the work you do; or you will take up some form of learning or employment to please a relative.

QUEEN OF CLUBS (inquirer) relatives have a great influence in your life; or your life is influenced by early home training; or you have nice relatives.

JACK OF CLUBS (relatives) you will be surrounded by many relatives; and new ones will be added from time to time. If not relatives, you have many friends.

TEN OF CLUBS (journey) some of your relatives are going away on a trip or are coming to your home from a distance; or you will lose them or a close friend by their moving away; or you will visit some relatives.

NINE OF CLUBS (luck) you should have lucky relatives; or through some of your relatives you will be lucky.

EIGHT OF CLUBS (achievement) some achievements will come through people related to you.

SEVEN OF CLUBS (messages) you will receive a message from a relative or friend who invites you to a party or christening; or a pleasant phone call.

Every baby born into the world is a finer one than the last.

—Charles Dickens

Spade Suit

ACE OF SPADES (death) the death of a relative is near and you will hear of it soon; or one has recently passed on. Could be a divorce in the family.

KING OF SPADES (callers) relatives will call. Be on your guard in any conversation with them; or you have a relative on the police force or in some public service who calls on you.

QUEEN OF SPADES (gratitude) you have a few grateful relatives; also they may hinder your progress as you may have to support them. Always remember a grateful friend is worth more than money; or you will be grateful to a friend or relative.

JACK OF SPADES (compass-thoughts) a relative is not strictly honest. To your face such people are very charming, but their thoughts are not upright; or a young relative may be employed in the media.

TEN OF SPADES (sun) a relative informs you about an estate other relatives were trying to keep from you; or the uncovering of something you should know comes late in the evening or at night.

NINE OF SPADES (disappointment) your relatives are a worthless lot; or relatives that you know nothing about will put in an appearance if you become wealthy or famous; or a great loss through a relative; or you will or have lost a relative by death.

EIGHT OF SPADES (trouble) relatives will cause trouble; or will help you out of trouble; or you worry about them.

SEVEN OF SPADES (health) relatives will make you sick at heart through the way they treat you or act; or are concerned about someone's health.

House of Health

Heart Suit

ACE OF HEARTS (the abode) in the House of Health indicates that your home environment has much to do with the way you feel. Also indicates no sickness in the home for some time to come; also, if there is someone ill at home now, this will be eliminated soon.

KING OF HEARTS (enjoyment) either the recovery of some person who has been ill makes you happy; or through the right thinking and management you are well and strong; or you enjoy good health.

QUEEN OF HEARTS (friends) you will hear good news regarding a friend's or a relative's health.

JACK OF HEARTS (popularity) illness may come to you or to someone dear to you because of overwork; or you will hear of the illness of some famous person—relative, friend, or prominent person unknown to you.

TEN OF HEARTS (marriage or union) you will hear of a wedding that makes you sick at heart; or there will be a uniting of something in your community that will be for the betterment of the public's health.

NINE OF HEARTS (your wish) if you wished for good health, you shall have it; also indicates you should be blessed with good health; a long life.

EIGHT OF HEARTS (moon-love) you should have a very strong heart and good lungs. Healthy loved ones.

SEVEN OF HEARTS (happiness) good health brings you happiness. Also worry can cause you to be nervous. Don't worry; concentrate on what you want.

Diamond Suit

ACE OF DIAMONDS (new undertaking) if you have had poor health in the past, something will change this condition. If in good health, don't work too hard or start anything that would drain on your vitality, be moderate; or new medical treatments.

KING OF DIAMONDS (legal papers) if you have a sedentary job, be sure you exercise; also indicates a bilious condition. You may visit a dentist or doctor.

QUEEN OF DIAMONDS (seasons) your health is bettered by plenty of outdoor exercise, you may suffer from a headache if you neglect this. If ailing, you will improve.

JACK OF DIAMONDS (letters) you will receive hasty news in regards to someone's health; or a pamphlet will be sent to you, if ill, that you should read; or a doctor is called by phone.

TEN OF DIAMONDS (money) through money you will enjoy good health—by traveling and taking life easy. This applies mostly to elderly people. If ailing, money may pay for necessary treatment; or by working hard and making money, you will have good health.

NINE OF DIAMONDS (surprises) something you hear about someone's health; will surprise you; also about the birth of a child which surprises you.

EIGHT OF DIAMONDS (inheritance) you have inherited good health; if ailing, through someone's aid or treatment, you will recover your health.

SEVEN OF DIAMONDS (success) your health affects your success. Be careful of your health and you will succeed. Good health and success indicated.

Club Suit

ACE OF CLUBS (gift) a gift you receive will benefit your health; something for garden or out-of-door work.

KING OF CLUBS (vocation) your health will have something to do with your work; also indicates worry can do more harm than an ailment. If a doctor, many patients.

QUEEN OF CLUBS (inquirer) you should have good health for many years to come. If ill, a speedy recovery is in sight.

JACK OF CLUBS (relatives) you will be much concerned over the health of a relative or a close friend; also indicates danger in the street; or you have healthy relatives or they run a nursing home.

TEN OF CLUBS (journey) a relative will take a trip to benefit his health; or you will take a trip that is a benefit to your health; or a change of environment or condition.

NINE OF CLUBS (luck) you have good luck and good health in store for you. If a nurse, good luck through a patient.

EIGHT OF CLUBS (achievement) your business should be connected with the public's health in some way; or your health will have something to do with your business or work; or work in a hospital.

SEVEN OF CLUBS (messages) you will receive a message regarding someone's health or recovery; or a message about an accident. If a doctor or nurse, many phone calls.

> *Look to your Health; and if you have it, praise God, and value it next to a good conscience; for health is the second blessing that we mortals are capable of; a blessing that money cannot buy.*

—Izaak Walton

Spade Suit

ACE OF SPADES (death) you should be careful with your health; if you are doing dangerous work, be careful; also indicates a short sick spell; or ill health to a close relative.

KING OF SPADES (callers) callers have something to do with your health, like a doctor; or you are taking treatments that will improve your health; or you will take healthful out-of-door exercise; or a caller that is not well.

QUEEN OF SPADES (gratitude) you have been instrumental in helping someone keep well or get well; and they will be very ungrateful.

JACK OF SPADES (compass-thoughts) you may wonder if a different climate will make you feel better; or if thinking of making a change in residence, you may wonder if you will feel well where you are going; or you are wondering where to go on a vacation; or you will hear of health treatments that interest you.

TEN OF SPADES (sun) plenty of sunshine and fresh air will do more for your health than all medicines and doctors put together, if you are ailing try this. Also be careful in the street at night; or if ailing you will take light treatments.

NINE OF SPADES (disappointment) you have been sick or had a loss through someone's illness; also indicates an upset mental condition caused by work you dislike or the people around you. Cheer up—this will change.

EIGHT OF SPADES (trouble) a sick spell caused by the loss of someone you loved; or you worry about your health or the health of someone else; trouble or sickness or an accident is indicated; or you fret over something you neglect.

SEVEN OF SPADES (health) you should have good health for some time to come. If a doctor or nurse, you will be very busy.

House of Money

Heart Suit

ACE OF HEARTS (the abode) in the House of Money indicates that money comes from home; or some work done at home will bring money; or you will sell your home if you own it. Money comes through a home condition.

KING OF HEARTS (enjoyment) a large sum of money comes to you through the efforts of another, like a father, uncle, or a dear friend; or a business transaction brings you enjoyment. Good business for amusement places—summer resort or theatre, etc.

QUEEN OF HEARTS (friends) a friend will give a loan or help you make money. Also indicates friendly cooperation from employer or employees.

JACK OF HEARTS (popularity) through being well liked money will be given to you; or you will earn it through a talent; or it comes through being popular; or through something that is in popular demand with the public.

TEN OF HEARTS (marriage or union) through a marriage you will make big money. If married, your mate will be a great help to you; also indicates the union of something that brings big money in business.

NINE OF HEARTS (your wish) if you have wished for money, you will get it; or your wish is hindered by the lack of money. A good chance for your wish.

EIGHT OF HEARTS (moon-love) through someone who loves you, you will receive much money; also, if single, love and money come into your life. A wealthy marriage.

SEVEN OF HEARTS (happiness) through the receipt of some money, you will buy something you want, and it will give you much happiness.

> Proud of your money you may strut,
> But fortune does not change your birth.
>
> —Horace

Diamond Suit

ACE OF DIAMONDS (new undertaking) money will come through a new undertaking. Take advantage of any offer—work or investment.

KING OF DIAMONDS (legal papers) some money that comes through a paper will need the services of an attorney; also an opportunity to invest. Stocks, bonds, or loans.

QUEEN OF DIAMONDS (seasons) you will receive money shortly, either through investment or work. There is money here for you. If making a loan on time payments, you will succeed.

JACK OF DIAMONDS (letters) you will receive hasty news concerning money; also you wish for money but never give a thought as to how it is earned; or mail brings money.

TEN OF DIAMONDS (money) you will receive a large sum of money; or an opportunity is coming your way to make a loan or change one to less interest; or a debt paid of long standing; a sure sign of better money conditions; use this carefully.

NINE OF DIAMONDS (surprises) you will be surprised about an opportunity that will be offered which will better your position, where you will make more money. Take what is offered. It is good for you; or you will receive money unexpectedly.

EIGHT OF DIAMONDS (inheritance) you will inherit some money—small sum; also stocks and bonds. Legacies come from unlooked-for places at times and a person does not have to die for you to inherit; or a small gift of money.

SEVEN OF DIAMONDS (success) money matters will bring you success in the future. Concentrate on an opportunity that is present in the work. Success there for you.

Club Suit

ACE OF CLUBS (gift) you will receive a large sum of money or the equivalent; or the purchase of jewelry—something valuable.

KING OF CLUBS (vocation) if you are working, you can look for a raise in pay, better position, or good business; or more money from wherever your support comes from.

QUEEN OF CLUBS (inquirer) even though you may not know at this time where the money is coming from, you will surely make or receive some soon.

JACK OF CLUBS (relatives) you have a very wealthy relative or friend who will be or is very kind to you; or you will give some money to a relative or friend.

TEN OF CLUBS (journey) money comes to you from a distance; or through a trip or change of work you will make more money; a change for the better. This could be for the sale of land or a car. If in the racing business or transportation, money won or good business.

NINE OF CLUBS (luck) you should have good luck in money matters, such as choosing good stocks and knowing what to buy at the right time in the market. Money through a lucky gamble. This applies to anything.

EIGHT OF CLUBS (achievement) through some achievement you will make a large sum of money. Business and money are indicated—and work.

SEVEN OF CLUBS (messages) you will receive a message concerning a money making opportunity. Concentrate on any proposition that is offered within the week, as a talk about money over the phone or by mail.

Spade Suit

ACE OF SPADES (death) you will receive an inheritance, insurance, stocks, or bonds through a death; or by a change of some kind, you will benefit financially.

KING OF SPADES (callers) you will pay a fine; also an opportunity is lost here; or callers discuss money or a loan asked or you lay out plans with a caller.

QUEEN OF SPADES (gratitude) a grateful person will offer an investment that is in the primitive state like lumber, mining, etc. If so inclined, this will be to your benefit. Or if you are handling someone's estate for him, he may be very ungrateful for the investments you make; or you will be grateful for a debt paid.

JACK OF SPADES (compass-thoughts) money sometime in your life will come from many sources and from many directions. If in business, plenty of orders.

TEN OF SPADES (sun) the west will be a good place to make your investments. Golden opportunities await you. Indicates also investment in oil land or lumber—a good investment.

NINE OF SPADES (disappointment) you will have trouble over money, which you lose in real estate, worthless bonds, stocks, etc.; or you will meet with a loss of some other kind; a friend loss is indicated; or a delay in a note to be paid.

EIGHT OF SPADES (trouble) you will have trouble over money; also you should not take other people's advice when an opportunity presents itself; use your own good judgment. Do not worry over money.

SEVEN OF SPADES (health) you will lose money through sickness; your health has something to do with your money conditions. If a nurse or doctor, you will make money by someone's illness or someone who needs your care. Cheer up—health and money indicated.

House of Seasons

Heart Suit

ACE OF HEARTS (the abode) in the House of Seasons indicates that before the season changes you will have some change in your home—better conditions, new furniture, more rooms added, a move, or a vacation.

KING OF HEARTS (enjoyment) within a week you will hear something that brings great enjoyment; it will come through a person who has your welfare at heart.

QUEEN OF HEARTS (friends) friends will ask you to spend your vacation with them, or they will spend theirs with you; or you will set a time to meet a friend.

JACK OF HEARTS (popularity) if you are in the theatrical world, you will become famous before many seasons. Also if merchandising, your product will be in demand before long; or your services will be sought.

TEN OF HEARTS (marriage or union) if you are single and want to get married, you will have an offer before the year has passed. It also indicates that something in a business way will change hands this year—will benefit you financially.

NINE OF HEARTS (your wish) time has something to do with your wish; in time you will get it, as it takes time to get it.

EIGHT OF HEARTS (moon-love) single, before the next season has passed, you will have a new sweetheart; or you will make a new friend who will benefit you.

SEVEN OF HEARTS (happiness) before the present season is past, you will meet with happiness. Be ready to receive the good things that come your way.

> There is a time for some things,
> And a time for all things;
> A time for great things
> And a time for small things.
>
> —Miguel de Cervantes

Diamond Suit

ACE OF DIAMONDS (new undertaking) if you recently started in some new enterprise or undertaking of some kind, be patient. It will take some time for it to develop; or within three months, something new in store for you.

KING OF DIAMONDS (legal papers) if you are expecting some legal papers at a certain date, they should arrive on time; indication that you will have something to do with time and legal papers here, like a note to be paid by a certain date; or some court action will be set for a certain date.

QUEEN OF DIAMONDS (seasons) whatever you wished for will take about three months to get or complete.

JACK OF DIAMONDS (letters) if you are expecting hasty news, it will be delayed. Or you should answer your mail promptly.

TEN OF DIAMONDS (money) if you are expecting some money to be paid, in time this will happen. There is a delay here; or money received monthly.

NINE OF DIAMONDS (surprises) a surprise is due you in nine days; this will be a good surprise.

EIGHT OF DIAMONDS (inheritance) an inheritance will come to you from an elderly person; or if you have an inheritance coming, it will be several seasons before you receive your share. Money will be paid to you.

SEVEN OF DIAMONDS (success) it will take seven days, weeks, or months before you meet with success in something you expect. But better success as time goes on.

Club Suit

ACE OF CLUBS (gift) you will soon receive a gift that you have long desired; or time set for the sale of property or a standing offer will be presented.

KING OF CLUBS (vocation) if you are working or going into something new, you will be employed for a long time. If taking an examination for a position, you shall get it.

QUEEN OF CLUBS (inquirer) before this season has passed, you should have something come your way that will be of great benefit to you; a change of some kind.

JACK OF CLUBS (relatives) some relatives or friends want you to spend your time with them; or you waste your time in some way. Do more for yourself.

TEN OF CLUBS (journey) you will make a change or take a trip before this season is passed. Plan for this change that is to take place.

NINE OF CLUBS (luck) good luck will visit you before this season is passed.

EIGHT OF CLUBS (achievement) it will take some time for you to achieve in business or in any pursuit you follow; or better business in the next three months—a business deal.

SEVEN OF CLUBS (messages) a hurried message comes to you, maybe from an old person; or someone asks you to hurry and meet him; a message involving time; or you will talk about future plans by phone.

> *Our seasons have no fixed returns,*
> *Without our will they come and go;*
> *At noon our sudden summer burns,*
> *Ere sunset all is snow.*

—James Russell Lowell

Spade Suit

ACE OF SPADES (death) you will lose a dear friend by death before this season has passed; or a change of condition comes into your life in the next three months by ridding yourself of an annoying condition. Lucky day—Monday.

KING OF SPADES (callers) you will have many new callers in a short time; newly made friends, or a caller will come to show you property or some large object for you to purchase. Lucky day—Tuesday.

QUEEN OF SPADES (gratitude) you are undecided in what you want to do; nothing seems right. If friends want to help, you think they are wrong; if you are not in that state of mind, just drifting, you will be soon. Concentrate and snap out of it, as a grateful person will pay you a call or visit.

JACK OF SPADES (compass-thoughts) you will be very undecided in something you want to do; or make a move in the direction or place you want to live in. Lucky day—Wednesday.

TEN OF SPADES (sun) the next three months should change conditions in your life; or through the past three months things have changed for you, perhaps so gradually that you have not noticed it. The sun should shine for you the next three months. Lucky day—Thursday.

NINE OF SPADES (disappointment) you are disappointed with something, either the location you live in or the place you work; disappointment is indicated strongly. A delayed appointment. Lucky day—Friday.

EIGHT OF SPADES (trouble) before three months pass, you will have some obstacle to surmount; trouble is indicated strongly. Do not worry—time eliminates all annoying conditions. Lucky day—Saturday.

SEVEN OF SPADES (health) if you are ailing or someone in your immediate family is sick, a change in environment will help you. Good health indicated. Lucky day—Sunday.

House of Friends

Heart Suit

ACE OF HEARTS (the abode) in the House of Friends indicates that your friends love you and your home; and they can always find the welcome sign on the door; or a friend will help you secure a home.

KING OF HEARTS (enjoyment) if your friends want real enjoyment they call on you or take you with them; also, a kindly person will see that you enjoy some place of amusement.

QUEEN OF HEARTS (friends) you should have one friend who will always stick to you throughout your life. Friendly help.

JACK OF HEARTS (popularity) you have or will have the friendship of a very noted or famous person; or through friends you will become famous.

TEN OF HEARTS (marriage or union) a very dear friend will ask your hand in marriage, if a widow or widower; or one of your dearest friends will get married; also indicates the union of old friends, or schoolmates.

NINE OF HEARTS (your wish) a friend will intercede and help you get your wish if he possibly can; or a friend has something to do with what you wish for or about; or a new person you meet will help you.

EIGHT OF HEARTS (moon-love) you will receive love and esteem from your neighbors, fellow workers, or employees; and a friend will do you a good deed without your knowledge.

SEVEN OF HEARTS (happiness) friends will have much to do with your future happiness. Cultivate good friends; avoid jealousy.

> *There are three faithful friends—an old wife, an old dog,*
> *and ready money.*
>
> —Benjamin Franklin

Diamond Suit

ACE OF DIAMONDS (new undertaking) you can expect moral support from friends in a new business or undertaking; also, you may go into a new undertaking with a friend. Cooperation indicated.

KING OF DIAMONDS (legal papers) you will have the protection of professional persons in time of need. They will help you in a court action or anything you cannot decide for yourself in a legal way. Or a fine doctor will help if his services are needed or you sign a paper with a friend.

QUEEN OF DIAMONDS (seasons) in your lifetime you will have a very wealthy friend on whom you can depend and you benefit by it. Financial gains or good advice from this party.

JACK OF DIAMONDS (letters) hasty news will come asking for money; or you will be asked in a hasty way for a loan. Remember borrowers do not remain friends; or a friendly letter arrives.

TEN OF DIAMONDS (money) through a friend you will be put in a position whereby you will make some money or gain in some way; or you will have prosperous friends.

NINE OF DIAMONDS (surprises) a surprise comes from a friend—a good surprise, like a surprise party, birthday party; or you will do something that will surprise your friends.

EIGHT OF DIAMONDS (inheritance) you will inherit something of value from a friend; or a small sum of money will be given you.

SEVEN OF DIAMONDS (success) you will either get a new position or work for a friend; friends will influence your future success.

Club Suit

ACE OF CLUBS (gift) you have a special gift for making friends; also indicates that friends will help you get a start in the world; or a nice gift from a friend.

KING OF CLUBS (vocation) a friend will either help you get a position or influence you in what you do; or the people you work with are good friends.

QUEEN OF CLUBS (inquirer) you should have many friends; or a dear friend wants to help and protect you. A new and lovely friend will be made soon.

JACK OF CLUBS (relatives) you have a relative who will prove a real friend in time of need; or a relative will befriend you when you are not present.

TEN OF CLUBS (journey) you are going to make a change in friends; or by a trip you make new friends; change of some kind; or you visit a friend; or a friend visits you.

NINE OF CLUBS (luck) through a friend you will have much good luck, or some friend you have is lucky for you.

EIGHT OF CLUBS (achievement) through a friend you will get something you want, or friends will help you get it—in business, work; or an achievement of some kind.

SEVEN OF CLUBS (messages) a message from a friend will bring good financial news; or a friend buys your business if you have one for sale or helps you with it. A talk of business by phone.

> *Friendship is the great chain of human society, and intercourse of letters is one of the chiefest links of that chain.*
> —James Howell

Spade Suit

ACE OF SPADES (death) some time in your life, you will have a friend who is in the slaughterhouse business, undertaker, casket maker, or some business pertaining to the dead; or you may lose a friend by death.

KING OF SPADES (callers) a friend will help you or call when you need encouragement most; or an officer of the law will befriend you. A friendly help is indicated.

QUEEN OF SPADES (gratitude) one good friend is worth more than a dozen others; also use your own judgment on some proposition that is coming up next week.

JACK OF SPADES (compass-thoughts) you should not be too trusting; all are not friends. Also someone who pretends to be a friend will not be faithful and will cause trouble; or you will hear a friend talk on the radio or TV.

TEN OF SPADES (sun) something will be presented that sounds like a good investment—the pot of gold at the end of the rainbow that will turn out to be brass. Be careful; this will come through a friend who really thinks this is a good investment. Investigate any offer well.

NINE OF SPADES (disappointment) you will lose a friend; or a loss through an investment a friend recommended; also borrowers don't remain friends very long; or angry words with someone.

EIGHT OF SPADES (trouble) trouble is caused by friends. Be careful; select good company; or you will help a friend in need; or friends will talk their troubles over with you.

SEVEN OF SPADES (health) the health of a friend will concern you very much; or a good friend will help you regain your health if you are ill; or you have a kind friend who is a nurse or doctor.

House of Gifts

Heart Suit

ACE OF HEARTS (the abode) in the House of Gifts indicates that you will receive a gift to use in your abode, like furniture, art objects, or something useful.

KING OF HEARTS (enjoyment) you will receive a gift from someone who has your best interests at heart; something you will enjoy very much; or you give enjoyment to others by making or giving them things.

QUEEN OF HEARTS (friends) a friend will bring you a beautiful gift, something you have wanted for a long time.

JACK OF HEARTS (popularity) you will receive a gift by entering some popular contest, like an ad on the radio or in the paper. If you haven't entered into such competition, do so and win. If young, an offer made to do something nice in front of the public—because you merit it.

TEN OF HEARTS (marriage or union) you will either give a wedding present or receive one. If married, an anniversary present, or a graduation or birthday present.

NINE OF HEARTS (your wish) if you wished for a gift, you will receive it, as soon as it is possible for the other party to afford to give it. If you want to find a certain article for a gift you will locate it—or find out what is wanted.

EIGHT OF HEARTS (moon-love) you will receive a gift from your sweetheart, if single; or a gift from a very dear friend; or a gift from members of the family.

SEVEN OF HEARTS (happiness) a gift you receive will give you great happiness, like a radio, musical instrument; something you will enjoy very much. Could be a new home or car.

> *Every good gift and every perfect gift is from above, and cometh down from the Father of light, with whom is no variableness, neither shadow or turning.*
>
> —James I, 17

Diamond Suit

ACE OF DIAMONDS (new undertaking) an undertaking will be offered, like a gift in appreciation for a favor of long standing; or a merit or award—or you will make gifts.

KING OF DIAMONDS (legal papers) you will receive a gift of a deed, bonds or stocks or something that comes on paper; or you will have to employ an attorney to keep a gift that has been given to you; or a doctor will give you good advice.

QUEEN OF DIAMONDS (seasons) something you desire very much will be given you this season; or a present from an elderly person. A lasting gift will be received.

JACK OF DIAMONDS (letters) you will receive hasty news about a gift you will receive; or a gift of flowers or music.

TEN OF DIAMONDS (money) you will receive an unexpected gift of quite a sum of money.

NINE OF DIAMONDS (surprises) a surprise about a gift you will receive; a gift of clothing or something personal is indicated.

EIGHT OF DIAMONDS (inheritance) you will inherit something, or it will be given to you and you will share this gift with others. To inherit means to receive.

SEVEN OF DIAMONDS (success) some gifts you receive soon will help you in your line of work—a new typewriter, car—something you can use in your work, if a housewife, something for the home; or successful business when merchandise is sold, or an offer made to your advantage.

> *Give, and it shall be given unto you; good measure, pressed down, and shaken together, and running over.*

—Luke VI, 38

Club Suit

ACE OF CLUBS (gift) you will receive a long desired gift; something very lovely and useful; or a large sum of money. Many nice gifts in store for you.

KING OF CLUBS (vocation) your employer, or someone where you attend school or work, will present you with a gift; or someone will give you a gift for a favor you have bestowed; or an offer to make something small that can be given as a premium or a gift of a premium.

QUEEN OF CLUBS (inquirer) you will receive an unexpected gift, something personal like wearing apparel; or something you will personally use; or a gift of money.

JACK OF CLUBS (relatives) you may expect a gift from a close friend or relative, a small gift you have long desired; or a friend or relative will remember you in his will.

TEN OF CLUBS (journey) you will receive a gift from afar; or a package you sent for arrives.

NINE OF CLUBS (luck) you will be lucky in receiving a gift, either you win it or you find something and can't find the owner.

EIGHT OF CLUBS (achievement) through an achievement you will receive a gift; or if in business, you will improve your sales by giving premiums, or you will manufacture articles that will be used as gifts, or an offer of partnership.

SEVEN OF CLUBS (messages) someone calls you by phone and tells you of a gift he has for you; or people call to show you a gift, like a new automobile, or something they can bring to you; or a gift from a radio program.

Spade Suit

ACE OF SPADES (death) through a death you will receive a gift; or you will dislike something that is given you and you either exchange it or give it away; or you will send flowers for a funeral.

KING OF SPADES (callers) someone will call and give you something you dislike or don't want; or a court order in your favor. If in the military, promotion coming.

QUEEN OF SPADES (gratitude) someone will give you a gift because he is grateful; or an ungrateful person will try to keep someone from giving you something promised you. A grateful person will be glad to receive some of your unwanted clothes.

JACK OF SPADES (compass-thoughts) a deceitful person will give you something then talk about you afterwards. This person's thoughts are for their own gain. Be careful of quality when you shop.

TEN OF SPADES (sun) you will receive a gift that has long been delayed; or an investment in oil or mining turns out well.

NINE OF SPADES (disappointment) a gift when received is not pleasing to you; or it has been damaged in delivery; or you will be disappointed in not receiving a promised gift; or some clothing or purchase is not of the quality you thought when purchasing it. A loss through inferior merchandise; or delay in delivery.

EIGHT OF SPADES (trouble) trouble will arise over a gift; or in settling an estate.

SEVEN OF SPADES (health) a gift you receive will improve your health, or will keep you in good health; or you are blessed with a gift of good health; or someone you have helped regarding his health will give you a gift; or you will improve your health through prescribed routine.

House of Letters

Heart Suit

ACE OF HEARTS (the abode) in the House of Letters indicates that you will receive a letter, if away from your loved ones, that tells the news of home; or a letter telling you about a friend or relative building or moving into a new home. This letter will contain news of some kind about a home; or a home for you.

KING OF HEARTS (enjoyment) you will receive a letter that you will enjoy reading from someone who has your best interests at heart; or an invitation to an enjoyable affair.

QUEEN OF HEARTS (friends) you will receive good news from a friend. A letter telling you nice things.

JACK OF HEARTS (popularity) you will write something that makes you become popular; or you receive a letter because you are popular, desiring your services. If in the theatrical world, a letter from your agent.

TEN OF HEARTS (marriage or union) you will receive an invitation to a wedding; or you will mail wedding invitations; or receive a letter telling you of a wedding; or a business document—or you will mail same.

NINE OF HEARTS (your wish) if your wish was about receiving a letter, you will get it; or you will receive a letter in regards to your wish.

EIGHT OF HEARTS (moon-love) if single, you will receive a letter from someone who loves you; or a letter that brings good news.

SEVEN OF HEARTS (happiness) you will receive some good news soon that brings happiness with it; should be within seven days.

Diamond Suit

ACE OF DIAMONDS (new undertaking) a letter comes very soon regarding a new undertaking, like a friend offering you a share in his business; or a new position offered; or you send out business announcement advertising.

KING OF DIAMONDS (legal papers) a paper will come through the mail for you to sign; or a letter concerning a legal action; or there is an important letter coming to you; or a deed, lease, contract, will—a legal paper; or you will receive an announcement of the opening of a new law office or doctor's office.

QUEEN OF DIAMONDS (seasons) you should not put off answering letters; someone awaits word from you; or you are anxious to hear from a certain person. You should receive plenty of mail the next three months.

JACK OF DIAMONDS (letters) you will receive a letter. The news will be very important to you, and when you receive it, you will be left wondering just what to do. Concentrate here; it will be like news of someone wanting you to come to them, etc. Look for a message.

TEN OF DIAMONDS (money) a letter you receive will contain money or a check; or someone will ask for a loan in a letter—use your best judgment here.

NINE OF DIAMONDS (surprises) you will be surprised to receive a letter from someone you least expect; or an invitation.

EIGHT OF DIAMONDS (inheritance) you will receive a letter telling of an inheritance; or it will contain a small amount of money; or money paid by money order.

SEVEN OF DIAMONDS (success) through the receipt of a letter, you will succeed in something you are doing or want to do. This may offer employment, if out of work. If employed as a secretary, you will have plenty of mail to answer.

Club Suit

ACE OF CLUBS (gift) you will receive a gift through the mail, like a subscription for a magazine; or a book or money order; or you will send money by mail.

KING OF CLUBS (vocation) you will be offered work in a letter; or you read about someone getting a good position; or letters or mail may influence your present work. Advertising indicated.

QUEEN OF CLUBS (inquirer) a very personal letter comes to you soon; or you have just received one and are pondering over it. Plenty of mail in store for you.

JACK OF CLUBS (relatives) relatives want you to write; or you receive a long delayed letter from a relative or close friend; or you will be asked to read someone's letter.

TEN OF CLUBS (journey) you will receive a letter from across the water; or you will send one; or you take a long trip after receiving a letter; or someone invites you to make a trip.

NINE OF CLUBS (luck) you receive a long letter bringing you luck; or you write a letter in competition and win a contest; or good luck.

EIGHT OF CLUBS (achievement) through an achievement you are lucky; or a letter asks you to go to work.

SEVEN OF CLUBS (messages) you will receive a letter; also sudden news of some kind regarding papers. Long distance call or message read over the phone.

> *Carrier of news and knowledge,*
> *Instrument of trade and industry,*
> *Promoter of mutual acquaintance,*
> *Of peace and good will among men and nations.*

> —Charles W. Ellot
> *inscription on southwest corner*
> *of Post Office, Washington, DC*

Spade Suit

ACE OF SPADES (death) you will receive a letter about a death; or a divorce or separation—or someone leaving their family to live in a new location.

KING OF SPADES (callers) a caller will bring news that really does not interest you; also a letter or bill collector to adjust a bill; or a court action will be received; or a caller asks you to read a paper.

QUEEN OF SPADES (gratitude) an ungrateful person will ask your opinion regarding a difficulty, or asks that you make a decision. Be careful what you write in a letter; let people make their own decisions; or you will be grateful to receive a certain letter.

JACK OF SPADES (compass-thoughts) you will receive a letter that annoys you; a letter from a spiteful person; or an unjust bill; something disturbing; or plenty of mail if in business—good publicity—or radio work or advertising or a contest won on the radio.

TEN OF SPADES (sun) you will receive a letter that will bring sunshine into your life; or if you have made an investment, it will bring returns, enabling you to take a nice trip or vacation; or a better income through investment.

NINE OF SPADES (disappointment) you will receive a letter telling you of a loss; or you will lose money on an investment away from here; or a loss of a letter in the mail; or you will be disappointed in not receiving word from someone.

EIGHT OF SPADES (trouble) you will receive a letter threatening trouble; trouble over a letter you write; a worry of some kind; or someone pours out his troubles in a letter to you—answer cheerfully.

SEVEN OF SPADES (health) you will receive a letter telling you about someone's health or inquiring about your own. This letter is important in some way; it may be a diet list or health magazine.

House of Trouble

Heart Suit

ACE OF HEARTS (the abode) in the House of Trouble indicates that worry or confusion in the home or angry words makes you miserable; or trouble over finding a place to live or purchase.

KING OF HEARTS (enjoyment) some trouble or worry will come your way, but you will be helped by a kindly person who has your welfare at heart.

QUEEN OF HEARTS (friends) you will hear of a friend in trouble whom you will aid; or friendly help.

JACK OF HEARTS (popularity) you will hear something that has been said about you that makes you feel badly; or by doing something indiscreet you will become unpopular. Be careful.

TEN OF HEARTS (marriage or union) if married, you and your mate may have angry words; or a lover's quarrel; or a quarrel with friends. Remember we all have faults.

NINE OF HEARTS (your wish) you will worry about your wish or there is some obstacle in connection with it. This does not signify you do not get it; you might have some trouble after you get it, because there is something better by waiting.

EIGHT OF HEARTS (moon-love) there is trouble in love; with sweetheart, mate, friends, or children; or a dispute with a trifling employee—angry words.

SEVEN OF HEARTS (happiness) jealousy may cause you some trouble; also, indicates worry or trouble can come from this. Catty remarks indicated.

> *There are times when we cannot see one step ahead of us,*
> *but five years later we are eating and sleeping somewhere.*
>
> —Chrysis

Diamond Suit

ACE OF DIAMONDS (new undertaking) worry and trouble will come if you start a new undertaking at present; or you will worry with fear—do not be fearful of tomorrow.

KING OF DIAMONDS (legal papers) you will have some kind of trouble over papers; or you will have something happen that worries you, where the services of an attorney will be needed; or worry over misplacing valuable papers; or lawsuit over paper you have signed; or you dislike the dentist's work—or health treatments.

QUEEN OF DIAMONDS (seasons) you have something to worry over, are annoyed with older people. Don't worry; time will change this. Time eliminates everything; concentrate on knowing this will change.

JACK OF DIAMONDS (letters) you will receive a troublesome letter that worries you; an unjust bill; something disagreeable; or news of someone else in trouble—or a trial followed in the paper.

TEN OF DIAMONDS (money) you will have trouble in collecting money due you; or worry over money matters; or an indication of some money trouble. Cheer up—this will change soon.

NINE OF DIAMONDS (surprises) you will be surprised by being blamed for doing something you did not do; or by some trouble that you hear of; or by an obstacle to surmount.

EIGHT OF DIAMONDS (inheritance) you will have trouble over an inheritance gift; or over a delayed payment due—collection of money.

SEVEN OF DIAMONDS (success) you worry over your future. Don't do this; remember the birds and flowers are not greater than you and they are cared for. Or you worry because you have been obstructed in your desires. Just know you will have what is right for you.

Club Suit

ACE OF CLUBS (gift) you have trouble over a gift—it may be damaged in delivery. Or you fret over something you want badly; or about angry words over something you bought.

KING OF CLUBS (vocation) you have trouble where you work, in finding work; or regarding work. Relax and change this vibration.

QUEEN OF CLUBS (inquirer) some trouble is worrying you or will presently. Concentrate, overcome or avoid this. Relax, smile, this will pass away. Do not be anxious over anyone.

JACK OF CLUBS (relatives) some relative will cause trouble for you; or relatives or friends will be of great help to you.

TEN OF CLUBS (journey) you will have trouble on a trip; you may get a traffic ticket; or you may have car trouble; or you are undecided on making a trip. Make your decision, then do it.

NINE OF CLUBS (luck) some misunderstandings will turn out in your favor because you were right.

EIGHT OF CLUBS (achievement) you will have trouble with something you are making or studying or money trouble in business. Relax, change the vibration—watch this change.

SEVEN OF CLUBS (messages) a message will cause trouble; or you will be angry in a conversation over the phone.

> *As aromatic plants bestow*
> *No spicy fragrance while they grow;*
> *But crush'd or trodden to the ground,*
> *Diffuse their balmy sweets around.*

—Oliver Goldsmith

Spade Suit

ACE OF SPADES (death) trouble is in store through a death—not necessarily in your immediate family. It could be connected with business associates or where you work; or your teacher at school may die, delaying your studies. Worry and sorrow indicated.

KING OF SPADES (callers) trouble with the law. Be careful about speeding, or getting in with bad company, or with someone who is a troublemaker, or with someone who relates his troubles to you.

QUEEN OF SPADES (gratitude) friends you have helped are angry because they can't use you to better their welfare again. Indicates ungrateful people.

JACK OF SPADES (compass-thoughts) troublemaker tries to be nice to your face and carries news; a busybody; or you will hear of a bad disaster over the air.

TEN OF SPADES (sun) you have had money troubles lately; or trouble over a farm if you own one. Concentrate on what is causing worry. Remember in each life a little rain must fall before the sun shines.

NINE OF SPADES (disappointment) you have had or will have many disappointments or others' troubles hinder your progress. Take stock of your mental attitude; this may be the cause of your disappointment.

EIGHT OF SPADES (trouble) indicates trouble, worry, and the blues. Cheer up.

SEVEN OF SPADES (health) either you worry about being sick or you are ill; trouble with sickness is coming your way. Avoid this by taking care of your health. Or you are heartsick and blue; cheer up for better times are coming; or tears shed at a funeral.

> *Let us be of good cheer, however, remembering that*
> *the misfortunes hardest to bear are those which never come.*

—James Russell Lowell

House of Disappointment

Heart Suit

ACE OF HEARTS (the abode) in the House of Disappointment indicates that you have lost a home; or a loss of some kind in the home; or you dislike the place in which you live. Be careful and guard this loss. It can be avoided if a loss has not already taken place.

KING OF HEARTS (enjoyment) you will want to be kind and nice to someone and you will be disappointed in the outcome; or someone is disappointed in you.

QUEEN OF HEARTS (friends) you are disappointed in a friend or you will lose a friend. The loss is here.

JACK OF HEARTS (popularity) you are disappointed in some popularity you expected; or the loss of it; or you may become unpopular through your actions, deeds, or words. Guard what you do and say.

TEN OF HEARTS (marriage or union) you will be disappointed in the outcome of some wedding; or you will lose someone very dear to you through their marriage and moving away. If in business, a disappointment in regards to some progress that should have taken place and did not; or a delayed business conference.

NINE OF HEARTS (your wish) you would lose or be disappointed if you got your wish; or there is delay in getting your wish.

EIGHT OF HEARTS (moon-love) you will be disappointed in someone you love; or a broken engagement or divorce; or an engagement or divorce postponed.

SEVEN OF HEARTS (happiness) you will be invited on a party and the date canceled; or a disappointment in something that rightfully should bring you happiness.

Diamond Suit

ACE OF DIAMONDS (new undertaking) you will be disappointed if you enter a new deal. A loss in some kind of investment; or a delay that is best for you.

KING OF DIAMONDS (legal papers) you may lose a valuable paper and so cause yourself much trouble; or a loss where papers are concerned so much so that an attorney may be needed to adjust matters; or a tooth will need filling.

QUEEN OF DIAMONDS (seasons) time plays an important part in a disappointment, either a date broken or a lost friendship of long standing. A long delay indicated.

JACK OF DIAMONDS (letters) you will be disappointed in the contents of a letter you receive; or will be disappointed in not receiving some word important to you; or a letter comes telling you of another's loss.

TEN OF DIAMONDS (money) there is a disappointment in some money you should receive; or the collection of money; or your salary is cut by shorter hours; or a deal where you make a commission falls through. Loss of money is indicated here, like the loss from your purse. But sometimes loss brings gain later.

NINE OF DIAMONDS (surprises) you will be surprised and disappointed by the actions of someone you trust. But this is for your own good; sever relations here.

EIGHT OF DIAMONDS (inheritance) if you are expecting an inheritance, you will be disappointed at the amount you receive. Whatever is given will be of little value; or a loss to you; or a delay in settling an estate.

SEVEN OF DIAMONDS (success) you are or will be disappointed in your progress or success. Change your outlook on life—success here for you.

Club Suit

ACE OF CLUBS (gift) you will be disappointed in not receiving a promised gift, or it is damaged in delivery; or the theft of something valuable. Take care of your clothes.

KING OF CLUBS (vocation) you will be discouraged in your work; or you lose your position; or disappointment in business, such as a contract canceled. There is a disappointment in what you are doing or what someone close to you is doing. This disappointment affects your support in some way; or delay in finishing some work.

QUEEN OF CLUBS (inquirer) you have met with a severe loss or are worrying over a loss you anticipate. There is disappointment or a loss of some kind. Take care of your personal belongings—your purse, money, etc. Or you are delayed in what you want to do.

JACK OF CLUBS (relatives) you will be disgusted with some relatives; or a friend disappoints you.

TEN OF CLUBS (journey) you will be disappointed over a trip of some kind; or you feel badly because someone has to leave you to go on a trip.

NINE OF CLUBS (luck) a disappointment will turn out lucky for you; or by not doing something or going on a trip you expected, you avoid an accident or some other unpleasant happening.

EIGHT OF CLUBS (achievement) you will be disappointed in not achieving your goal; or a business disappointment turns out in your favor.

SEVEN OF CLUBS (messages) you will be disappointed in callers not arriving who promised to call; or the cancellation of a business conference; or someone phones you and tells you of their loss.

Spade Suit

ACE OF SPADES (death) you will be disappointed in relationships that have been severed; or a loss through a death. A sad disappointment.

KING OF SPADES (callers) you should be careful of your belongings that you don't lose something. You might call the police over a loss or go to court over a stolen car; or a caller tells you of his loss.

QUEEN OF SPADES (gratitude) a disappointing loss is indicated from an ungrateful person; perhaps someone will do his best to break up your home or make you lose your job. You will meet a spiteful person.

JACK OF SPADES (compass-thoughts) someone will try to mislead you in telling you a wrong address where to buy something or direct you wrong in some way. This will disturb and lose time for you. Deceit is indicated; or you will be annoyed with poor advertising on the air.

TEN OF SPADES (sun) you will be disappointed, but through the loss you will find out or gain knowledge that will be very beneficial to you later. Loss and gain is indicated. Buying stocks could be involved.

NINE OF SPADES (disappointment) you have or will be disappointed or suffer a severe loss. A tragedy may be near but can be averted; or you are thwarted (for your own good) in something you want to do.

EIGHT OF SPADES (trouble) worry and disappointment are in store for you if you have not had them already. Grasp trouble like nettles, it will not sting. Be careful of what you are doing, especially when you drive.

SEVEN OF SPADES (health) your health (or someone's) will bring delay or disappointment in your life; or money conditions will be affected by ill health; or you are unsettled and upset over these conditions.

House of Death

Heart Suit

ACE OF HEARTS (the abode) in the House of Death indicates that you should be careful of sickness in the home; or there has been someone ill recently who will recover; or you will redecorate and clean house.

KING OF HEARTS (enjoyment) you will hear of the death of someone you cared for; the party may be a relative.

QUEEN OF HEARTS (friends) you will hear of the death of a dear friend; or hear of the death of a prominent lady.

JACK OF HEARTS (popularity) you will hear of the death of a very popular or famous person.

TEN OF HEARTS (marriage or union) you will hear of the death of a young person or a newlywed; or the breaking up (for the best) of an old condition in your life—or changing of a partnership.

NINE OF HEARTS (your wish) your wish picks up with a death of someone connected with it; or through a death you either get your wish or you don't get it; or through the forsaking of an old condition, your wish is possible.

EIGHT OF HEARTS (moon-love) the death of someone you love will make you grieve; or someone you love will lose someone and you will share their sorrow; or there will be a broken engagement.

SEVEN OF HEARTS (happiness) you have lost a pet by death or theft and you are very unhappy. Neighborhood trouble, or the loss of someone in your immediate neighborhood.

> *Sunset and evening star*
> *And one clear call for me!*
> *And may there be no moaning at the bar*
> *When I put out to sea.*

—Alfred Lord Tennyson

Diamond Suit

ACE OF DIAMONDS (new undertaking) the death of someone indicates a new environment in your life; or by the death of someone a new undertaking is in store for you; or you will make an entirely new change.

KING OF DIAMONDS (legal papers) you will hear of the death of someone very prominent; or you will sign a death certificate; or arrangements will be made about a death and papers will be handled by you. Also indicates the death of a very prominent professional man; or you will release something to another by signing a paper.

QUEEN OF DIAMONDS (seasons) no deaths seem imminent in your immediate family for some time.

JACK OF DIAMONDS (letters) you will receive a letter concerning an operation on a friend or relative that may prove fatal; or hasty news telling you of a death.

TEN OF DIAMONDS (money) money should come to you through the death of someone; or you will be saved the expense of caring for someone who is ill.

NINE OF DIAMONDS (surprises) you will be surprised about an accident or death, maybe that of a close friend.

EIGHT OF DIAMONDS (inheritance) you will inherit money, or jewelry that pleases you, through the death of someone.

SEVEN OF DIAMONDS (success) through the death of someone, you will succeed—like taking their position at work. There is a benefit to you through this death; or you may change your plans completely.

> *Death stands above me, whispering low*
> *I know not what into my ear;*
> *Of his strange language all I know*
> *Is, there is not a word of fear.*

—Walter Savage Landor

Club Suit

ACE OF CLUBS (gift) through the death of someone you will receive a present; or through the severance of a disagreeable friendship—you will receive a gift of praise.

KING OF CLUBS (vocation) the death of someone may change your present occupation; a change of work is indicated; or the severance of an unpleasant working condition.

QUEEN OF CLUBS (inquirer) you should take great care of yourself as danger in the street, or a fall of some kind, is evident. Accidents can be avoided if you take special precautions wherever you go or whatever you do; or you will change your mode of living.

JACK OF CLUBS (relatives) you will hear of the death of a relative, or of an accident to a relative or a dear friend.

TEN OF CLUBS (journey) you will take a trip because of a death, or go to a funeral, or you move to another state.

NINE OF CLUBS (luck) through luck you or a friend or relative will escape injury.

EIGHT OF CLUBS (achievement) you will hear of the death of a close business associate; or you will change your work or business.

SEVEN OF CLUBS (messages) you will receive a message about a death and will send flowers; or hear of the sickness of a friend who is badly hurt but who will recover. A call on a sick person.

Spade Suit

ACE OF SPADES (death) you will witness an accident where someone is killed; or you may be involved in an accident. Drive carefully and avoid this.

KING OF SPADES (callers) a caller will die shortly after talking to you; or a policeman calls regarding a death you know about; or a traffic accident.

QUEEN OF SPADES (gratitude) a suicide in your neighborhood that will affect you in some way; or someone may threaten suicide.

JACK OF SPADES (compass-thoughts) you are deceived in the health of someone you thought in perfect health—that person may die soon. That person knows he is ill but will not tell you; or you will hear news of a death on radio or TV.

TEN OF SPADES (sun) the sun will shine in your life after a certain person passes on; perhaps you know what is in store here or who the party is. Or the severance of a relationship.

NINE OF SPADES (disappointment) a great loss by death; or you have had a great loss by death; or a delay in hearing of a death.

EIGHT OF SPADES (trouble) you worry for fear someone you love will die; or you are grieving or will grieve over a death of a loved one—perhaps a pet.

SEVEN OF SPADES (health) someone's health or your own will improve with the death of someone; or you are blue and sick and wish death would relieve this condition; or you need diversion—go places, see people.

House of Undertaking

Heart Suit

ACE OF HEARTS (the abode) in the House of Undertaking indicates that you will be offered a new undertaking that can be started in your home; or you will build or remodel a home.

KING OF HEARTS (enjoyment) a very fine gentleman will offer to take you in on a new undertaking—his intentions are good and this seems to be to your advantage. Concentrate here. A good proposition to your advantage.

QUEEN OF HEARTS (friends) a friend will offer you a new undertaking. If you are wanting to do something, this should be a good opportunity.

JACK OF HEARTS (popularity) a new undertaking that is offered you should become popular and should prosper through the public's demand.

TEN OF HEARTS (marriage or union) a new undertaking along the lines of uniting either your services or business will be offered; this should be good. Or a new position is offered you. A contract signed.

NINE OF HEARTS (your wish) if you are looking to get into some business or work of some kind, you should get your wish.

EIGHT OF HEARTS (moon-love) if you are going into a new undertaking, be sure you like what you are going into; if you don't, you will fail or lose your job.

SEVEN OF HEARTS (happiness) a new undertaking that is offered will bring you happiness. This does not necessarily mean business or work—can be anything else. A new romance if single.

Your heart's desire be with you!

—William Shakespeare

Diamond Suit

ACE OF DIAMONDS (new undertaking) a new undertaking should prosper, or your present work should be successful. A positive sign when the card and house come together. Something good for your livelihood.

KING OF DIAMONDS (legal papers) you will sign a paper to enter partnership; or a new undertaking is in store. Everything should be in black and white if you go into partnership, or affiliate with some other firm.

QUEEN OF DIAMONDS (seasons) you will be offered a new undertaking with an older person. You will wait some time before you think it worthwhile.

JACK OF DIAMONDS (letters) a letter will come containing a new proposition; investigate well. Also something connected with studies through correspondence.

TEN OF DIAMONDS (money) soon you will make money by investments in a new company, patents, or an invention. Mining is a gamble but it will turn out well. Money made through a new venture.

NINE OF DIAMONDS (surprises) you will have a surprise concerning a new venture you are interested in or are offered. Something you learn to your advantage.

EIGHT OF DIAMONDS (inheritance) through an inheritance or gift, you will start a new undertaking; it will not bring a large sum of money. Or you may inherit a small income each month.

SEVEN OF DIAMONDS (success) a new venture will be offered, such as shares or commission. If attending school, part-time work will be offered you. Success is in store for you.

Club Suit

ACE OF CLUBS (gift) you may enter a business where gifts are sold or made; or you will make gifts for your friends and be known for your lovely work. A new business opportunity offered soon.

KING OF CLUBS (vocation) a new undertaking where you are employed would be to your advantage; something new for you; or a new opening in business.

QUEEN OF CLUBS (inquirer) soon you will enter a new undertaking, perhaps you know what it is now.

JACK OF CLUBS (relatives) you will benefit by a relative's new undertaking; or you and a relative will go into something new together.

TEN OF CLUBS (journey) you will enter into a business where machinery moves or something is in motion; or you travel in connection with your business; change and movement connected with a new venture.

NINE OF CLUBS (luck) a new venture will be lucky, go in and you will win.

EIGHT OF CLUBS (achievement) you will achieve much in your business if you start a new undertaking along the same line. A better job or a new business.

SEVEN OF CLUBS (messages) you will receive word about a new undertaking; or if you have started one, messages bring you business. Phone calls or advertising.

I have always recognized that the object of business is to make money in an honorable manner. I have endeavored to remember that the object of life is to do good.

—Peter Cooper

Spade Suit

ACE OF SPADES (death) a death will have something to do with a new undertaking; or if you start one, it will not prosper. Be sure to investigate a new job.

KING OF SPADES (callers) a caller will want you to enter into an investment, or business deal, or purchase something. Be careful for this might end up in court.

QUEEN OF SPADES (gratitude) some person will pretend to be grateful and want you to go into business, or will try to separate a husband and wife, or to break up a friendship. Be careful.

JACK OF SPADES (compass-thoughts) if you are going into a new undertaking, the outcome is doubtful. Be skilled in the particular line you enter. If you work in advertising—good new work for you.

TEN OF SPADES (sun) you should investigate a new undertaking before going into it. There is something you ought to look into and know about. Or you will study something that requires much research.

NINE OF SPADES (disappointment) you have had a loss over a new undertaking; or you will lose if you do start a new undertaking. Wait and investigate.

EIGHT OF SPADES (trouble) worry or trouble over a new undertaking. Concentrate and clear this up. This may not mean you, but it applies to your source of support. Do not fret over making a change—wait.

SEVEN OF SPADES (health) your health or someone else's plays an important part in a new undertaking; or you are heartsick and blue because you didn't take up some new undertaking that became successful; or, if a doctor, you may open a nursing home.

House of Achievement

Heart Suit

ACE OF HEARTS (the abode) in the House of Achievement indicates that you have been trained or are being trained at home for some achievement later in life; or you will achieve something at home; or your best achievement will be homemaking.

KING OF HEARTS (enjoyment) some achievement will bring you before the public; or through an achievement you will succeed; or, if young, you should strive for one thing and can be sure of a successful outcome in years to come; or you will enjoy great achievement.

QUEEN OF HEARTS (friends) you are going to enjoy some achievement of a friend—maybe social gains or acclaim of the public. Something nice is in store.

JACK OF HEARTS (popularity) you will receive much publicity through an achievement. Fame and fortune should be your lot in the near future through a new achievement.

TEN OF HEARTS (marriage or union) your best achievement comes through marriage; you will be a good homemaker or a good provider; or in business, your greatest achievement will come through getting more lines of merchandise to sell.

NINE OF HEARTS (your wish) if you have wished to achieve something, you will get your wish, but not as soon as you expected it.

EIGHT OF HEARTS (moon-love) your greatest achievement comes with the help of someone who loves you, or through any vocation that needs loving care.

SEVEN OF HEARTS (happiness) happiness is in store for you by mixing business with pleasure.

Diamond Suit

ACE OF DIAMONDS (new undertaking) some new undertaking will require hard work, but you will achieve much. Your best achievement lies in a brilliant career.

KING OF DIAMONDS (legal papers) if you are a professional person, you should achieve much; you should succeed where papers are connected with your work. Also some court order or patent papers may affect some achievement in the future.

QUEEN OF DIAMONDS (seasons) whatever you want to do, or are doing, will require time to achieve; also indicates some help from people older than yourself.

JACK OF DIAMONDS (letters) a letter or some form of learning from printed matter, like books, pamphlets, or school work, will influence your future achievements. Could be connected with flying an airmail plane or the delivery of something.

TEN OF DIAMONDS (money) your achievements will be many and will bring you money.

NINE OF DIAMONDS (surprises) you will try to do something you think impossible, and you will do this so well that you will surprise yourself. Never say I can't do that—I detest the word "can't."

EIGHT OF DIAMONDS (inheritance) through being clever or smart in some achievement, something good is offered you; or an inheritance is given you for being obedient to someone's wishes.

SEVEN OF DIAMONDS (success) some achievement brings big success in the future. Fame and fortune—try.

Club Suit

ACE OF CLUBS (gift) you will be helped through school by a gift of money; or you will achieve much through art or the making of gifts. Achievement through art.

KING OF CLUBS (vocation) your best achievement will come later in life; or all your achievements have come through hard work—mental or physical.

QUEEN OF CLUBS (inquirer) you will become an expert in some study you have taken up. This card tells that practice makes perfect; or you live a full life.

JACK OF CLUBS (relatives) one of your relatives will achieve much; or if you are young, your greatest achievements come after you leave your family.

TEN OF CLUBS (journey) you will be successful in business; also you may achieve success in publicity writing—something that goes into circulation.

NINE OF CLUBS (luck) through a piece of luck, you will find time or get the money to do something you like.

EIGHT OF CLUBS (achievement) as this card falls in its own house, you have achieved or will achieve much in the business world. Plenty for you to do.

SEVEN OF CLUBS (messages) if you are an artist or a professional person, you can expect many calls concerning your work—many clients or patients; a message will have something to do with your achievements. You would be a successful telephone operator.

> *If a man look sharply and attentively, he shall see fortune; for though she is blind she is not invisible.*
>
> —Francis Bacon

Spade Suit

ACE OF SPADES (death) you will sever connections with something soon that will help you to achieve something better. There is a decided change of some kind here.

KING OF SPADES (callers) someone will come to help you achieve something. There is outside help here; also indicates better achievements as you go along.

QUEEN OF SPADES (gratitude) some ungrateful person will try to block your progress; also if you have not been successful in your life, don't worry for you will succeed before you die.

JACK OF SPADES (compass-thoughts) you will be always dissatisfied with your achievements, always reaching for the moon or trying to perfect something all the time.

TEN OF SPADES (sun) your best work will be done in the afternoon; or that you do your planning at night, then carry out your plans when the sun shines.

NINE OF SPADES (disappointment) you are disappointed in something you are doing, or you are hindered in what you want to do. There is a loss indicated through this hindering. Change what is wrong.

EIGHT OF SPADES (trouble) you will have to surmount many obstacles before you reach your goal. Trouble in connection with achievement. You will win—try.

SEVEN OF SPADES (health) your health will have something to do with your achievements; or the health of someone else will affect you; or good health and achievement are in store for you.

House of Inheritance

Heart Suit

ACE OF HEARTS (the abode) in the House of Inheritance indicates that someone in the home will receive an inheritance, or the inheritance of a home. You can receive an inheritance without a death you know.

KING OF HEARTS (enjoyment) you will inherit valuable things from a relative or very close friend who has your welfare at heart; or a gift from a kindly person.

QUEEN OF HEARTS (friends) you will inherit some stocks, bonds, or personal property from a friend; or a beautiful personal gift will be received.

JACK OF HEARTS (popularity) by being popular with your friends or relatives, you will inherit some jewelry; or a Valentine sent on Valentine's Day.

TEN OF HEARTS (marriage or union) through marriage or the union of a partner you will inherit business shares or a life income; or you will be well provided for. Good income.

NINE OF HEARTS (your wish) your wish picks up with an inheritance, or by help from someone.

EIGHT OF HEARTS (moon-love) someone who loves you will remember you in a will; or you will receive a gift with love—perhaps flowers.

SEVEN OF HEARTS (happiness) you will have much jealousy over receiving a legacy. But in spite of this, you will have much happiness through the gain.

Diamond Suit

ACE OF DIAMONDS (new undertaking) you will enter a new undertaking through an inheritance left you; or a new undertaking brings unlooked-for opportunities and money.

KING OF DIAMONDS (legal papers) money should come to you through some person in the professional world; or you will sign someone's or your own will; or you will require the services of an attorney to take care of an inheritance for you. This may be settled out of court. Papers signed or handled involving money.

QUEEN OF DIAMONDS (seasons) an elderly person will pass away soon, and you will benefit thereby. This should happen within three months. A beneficial change.

JACK OF DIAMONDS (letters) you will receive a letter about an inheritance. It may be a gift from an aunt, or some close relative. This letter also will speak of her will. Or a letter bearing money.

TEN OF DIAMONDS (money) you will be remembered in a will and you should receive a large sum of money. Or a better income.

NINE OF DIAMONDS (surprises) you will be surprised about an inheritance you receive and never expected; a good surprise. A debt paid—or a loan or a gift.

EIGHT OF DIAMONDS (inheritance) as the card and house fall together this is a positive sign, and you will inherit something very soon. It may be a worthwhile gift from someone who is living, or at an early date someone who passes on will remember you in a will.

SEVEN OF DIAMONDS (success) you should succeed in settling an inheritance that is coming to you. Success and better income.

> We must take care to indulge only in such generosity as will help our friends and hurt no one—for nothing is generous, if it is not at the same time just.

> —Cicero

Club Suit

ACE OF CLUBS (gift) you will inherit a gift of stocks or bonds or personal belongings; or a raise in pay if working.

KING OF CLUBS (vocation) a gift of some kind helps you get work; or by an inheritance you go into business, school, or something you want to do; or you will administer an estate—or handle others' money for them.

QUEEN OF CLUBS (inquirer) you will fall heir to an estate; or you will be appointed administrator of an estate.

JACK OF CLUBS (relatives) you will inherit an estate from a relative; or a relative or friend will help you build an estate of your own.

TEN OF CLUBS (journey) you may lose an estate away from here that is rightfully yours because no effort was made to locate you; or an estate comes to you from a distance; or, if in real estate business, you will sell property that is away from your city of operations.

NINE OF CLUBS (luck) you will be lucky in winning some money, falling heir to an estate, or lucky in some way that a gift comes to you.

EIGHT OF CLUBS (achievement) through some achievement you will be well liked and left an estate—like a business or shares in a business; or you will be paid a bonus if you are an employee.

SEVEN OF CLUBS (messages) you will receive a message telling that you have inherited some money, a prize or something of the sort; or a message telling of someone else inheriting something; or a talk about a future investment possibility over the phone.

> *Money is welcome tho' it be in a dirty clout, but 'tis far more accept-*
> *able if it comes in a clean handkerchief.*

—James Howell

Spade Suit

ACE OF SPADES (death) you may inherit a fortune through a death; or the division of property with someone living.

KING OF SPADES (callers) someone calls to tell you of an inheritance; or you may be an administrator of an estate; or some court action comes with this estate or inheritance; or a loan repaid.

QUEEN OF SPADES (gratitude) a grateful person will leave you something in a will; also, you may give up an inheritance rather than go to court and fight over it.

JACK OF SPADES (compass-thoughts) someone thinks of you and envies you because you either have come into an inheritance or will, and they know about this. An envious person will be connected with an inheritance you receive; or jealous thoughts are sent your way because you are prosperous.

TEN OF SPADES (sun) through your sunny disposition and helpful ways, someone will remember you in a will. Remember money comes in the most unexpected ways.

NINE OF SPADES (disappointment) you will lose an inheritance that should rightfully be yours; or you will be disappointed in something that is left you in a will; or experience a delay in collecting a loan due or rent or royalties.

EIGHT OF SPADES (trouble) trouble comes over an inheritance; also bad feelings, worry, and tears indicated—perhaps you know what this is now.

SEVEN OF SPADES (health) you should have inherited good health; or you will be blue and heartsick over a death and an inheritance.

House of Callers

Heart Suit

ACE OF HEARTS (the abode) in the House of Callers indicates that someone will call where you live and surprise you by saying he has moved or bought a new home; or someone calls to show you property.

KING OF HEARTS (enjoyment) someone will call on you whom you are very happy to see—a person you love or like very much.

QUEEN OF HEARTS (friends) friends will call on you whom you haven't seen for a long time; or you will accidentally meet an old acquaintance in the street.

JACK OF HEARTS (popularity) someone calls upon you who is very noted.

TEN OF HEARTS (marriage or union) newlyweds will call on you; or a caller tells you about a wedding they attended.

NINE OF HEARTS (your wish) your wish has something to do with a call or callers.

EIGHT OF HEARTS (moon-love) someone will call on you who thinks a lot of you and whom you love—a love call.

SEVEN OF HEARTS (happiness) someone calls to see you very soon and brings much happiness to you.

The snow is lying very deep.
My house is sheltered from the blast.
I hear each muffled step outside,
I hear each voice go past.
But I'll not venture in the drift
Out of this bright security
Till enough footsteps come and go
To make a path for me.

—Agnes Lee

Diamond Suit

ACE OF DIAMONDS (new undertaking) a caller tells you of something he has accomplished; or someone will call on you to help you accomplish something; or a teacher calls to instruct you. Study indicated.

KING OF DIAMONDS (legal papers) a lawyer may call on you regarding some deal or have you sign a paper. There might be some court action involved here. A paper and a caller are involved. Also a call to a doctor inquiring about the health of a member of the family.

QUEEN OF DIAMONDS (seasons) old folks will call on you—maybe grandparents will come for a few months' visit; whoever the old folks are, they will want to spend some time with you, so be prepared. Or a time may be set for an appointment.

JACK OF DIAMONDS (letters) someone calls on you with a letter or paper for you to read; or a call about a letter sent to you.

TEN OF DIAMONDS (money) a caller tells you about a money investment. Look into this, as you will make some money; or someone might call on you to tell you of an investment that made him a large sum of money; or wealthy friends pay you a social visit.

NINE OF DIAMONDS (surprises) you will be paid a call that surprises you; a good surprise; be prepared.

EIGHT OF DIAMONDS (inheritance) someone will call on you soon regarding his inheritance; or one for yourself. Also look for callers at mealtimes; spongers or borrowers.

SEVEN OF DIAMONDS (success) a caller will tell of his or her success. Beware of beggars who turn out to be borrowers; or someone will call to congratulate you upon some wonderful success you have had.

Club Suit

ACE OF CLUBS (gift) you will receive a gift from someone who calls on you; or you will give a gift to a caller; or an agent calls and wants you to buy some household appliance.

KING OF CLUBS (vocation) if out of work, you will be employed where you have to make calls; work and calls are in store for you here; or a call for you to go to work.

QUEEN OF CLUBS (inquirer) you can expect callers soon; prepare for them as they will expect to be entertained.

JACK OF CLUBS (relatives) relatives will call on you.

TEN OF CLUBS (journey) you will make a social calling trip—one you have put off for a long time; or callers from a distance will arrive.

NINE OF CLUBS (luck) you will have good luck by calling on someone or by their calling on you. You find out something to your benefit.

EIGHT OF CLUBS (achievement) that callers will tell you of some business—some line they may want you to invest in or buy stock in. A business caller.

SEVEN OF CLUBS (messages) you can look for callers to congratulate you; or someone will inquire about your health; plenty of phone calls and mail are in store for you; or someone calls by phone telling you they are coming to see you.

> *We should render a service to a friend to bind him closer to us, and to an enemy to make a friend of him.*
>
> —Cleobulus

Spade Suit

ACE OF SPADES (death) callers will tell you of their illness; or you will visit a doctor, or he calls on you; or you will hear of a death through a caller.

KING OF SPADES (callers) many people will visit you soon. Indications are that you will be very busy receiving and entertaining your friends; or you will see people you are very anxious to see.

QUEEN OF SPADES (gratitude) ungrateful people you have helped will call and try to show off. A disagreeable caller. Be gracious and dismiss them.

JACK OF SPADES (compass-thoughts) friends will call and discuss plans for a trip. Beware of a new acquaintance who cannot be trusted; or you will receive a message.

TEN OF SPADES (sun) friends will call if the weather is nice; or because it is a nice day, they will call unexpectedly.

NINE OF SPADES (disappointment) you will be disappointed in people whom you entertain. Also indicates robbery or you will miss something after someone leaves. Take care; there is a loss through callers; or people you expect to call break their appointment.

EIGHT OF SPADES (trouble) callers cause trouble, like a tenant calls to say he cannot pay his rent or is moving; or angry words and trouble with a caller.

SEVEN OF SPADES (health) callers will tell how ill they have been or are and ask you to recommend a good doctor; or someone will call to tell you they have recovered from an illness.

House of Gratitude

Heart Suit

ACE OF HEARTS (the abode) in the House of Gratitude indicates that someone where you live is very grateful to you for what you do for him. There is gratitude shown about a home condition around you.

KING OF HEARTS (enjoyment) a person who loves you will be very grateful for any favors you give and will amply repay you at a later date.

QUEEN OF HEARTS (friends) friends are grateful or will be grateful for a favor you have done or will do for them; or you will be grateful to a friend for a favor.

JACK OF HEARTS (popularity) you will or have become popular among your friends because they are grateful for small favors you do.

TEN OF HEARTS (marriage or union) some newlyweds will be very grateful for something you do for them; or someone will be grateful to you for bringing old friends together again.

NINE OF HEARTS (your wish) your wish has something to do with gratitude, either on your part or someone else's; or you will be very grateful if you get your wish.

EIGHT OF HEARTS (moon-love) someone will be very grateful for something you have done and will remark they love you for your kindness.

SEVEN OF HEARTS (happiness) you will bring happiness into someone's life, and that person will be very grateful; or by your being grateful for small things, you will obtain much happiness.

> While I would fain to have some tincture of all the virtues, there is no quality I would rather have, and be thought to have, than gratitude. For it is not only the greatest virtue but even the mother of the rest.

—Cicero

Diamond Suit

ACE OF DIAMONDS (new undertaking) someone near you will be grateful for your help in some new undertaking; or you have a grateful friend.

KING OF DIAMONDS (legal papers) you will be grateful to someone for his help with some kind of papers; or you will help someone draw up a paper.

QUEEN OF DIAMONDS (seasons) someone is grateful for past favors and will repay you at a later date; time is involved here.

JACK OF DIAMONDS (letters) you will send a letter of condolence or of gratitude; or will receive one.

TEN OF DIAMONDS (money) someone will be grateful for your help financially—not necessarily the loan of money; or you will be grateful to someone who put something in your way that brought you money.

NINE OF DIAMONDS (surprises) you will be surprised when gratitude is shown you for a past favor you bestowed; this comes when you least expect it and need it most.

EIGHT OF DIAMONDS (inheritance) a position in business is sent your way by someone who is grateful to you for a past favor which you have forgotten about. Also could be an inheritance from a grateful friend or relative.

SEVEN OF DIAMONDS (success) your future success picks up with gratitude; or someone will be very grateful to you for your help in getting him a job or helping him to succeed.

Club Suit

ACE OF CLUBS (gift) you will be grateful for a gift you need very badly; or you will be thanked for help you give to a deserving person.

KING OF CLUBS (vocation) you will help someone with schoolwork or some other kind of work; a grateful friend in the business world or wherever you work.

QUEEN OF CLUBS (inquirer) someone will be grateful for a favor you bestow; or you will be grateful to someone for some past or future favor.

JACK OF CLUBS (relatives) you have grateful relatives or dear friends.

TEN OF CLUBS (journey) friends on a trip will be grateful for your help in getting them settled or for entertaining them; or you are grateful for a trip—or change of condition.

NINE OF CLUBS (luck) being grateful will bring you good luck. Show gratitude and honesty at all times.

EIGHT OF CLUBS (achievement) friends in the business world will be grateful and repay you at a later date; or you will receive a favor because you are grateful.

SEVEN OF CLUBS (messages) you will receive a message expressing gratitude; or you will receive a message you are grateful for.

> *Gratitude is a nice touch of beauty added last of all to the countenance, giving a classic beauty, an angelic loveliness, to the character.*

—Theodore Parker

Spade Suit

ACE OF SPADES (death) someone will be very grateful because you helped in time of need—at a funeral or death; or you will be grateful to friends for their help.

KING OF SPADES (callers) ungrateful people will call on you. If you know who these people are, treat them cool; it will be for your own good.

QUEEN OF SPADES (gratitude) someone you thought did not care for you will prove to be a real friend, and you will be very grateful for something he or she does for you.

JACK OF SPADES (compass-thoughts) you have trusted someone you never should have; or a bill collector calls and is very rude over an unjust bill.

TEN OF SPADES (sun) you find out about an injustice and save yourself from harm; also, a favor will be asked that you cannot grant.

NINE OF SPADES (disappointment) your kindness will meet with a disappointment or a loss. Choose friends carefully—we can't choose our relatives. Or something borrowed is not returned.

EIGHT OF SPADES (trouble) some kindness you have shown will meet with ingratitude. A supposed-to-be friend will be lost.

SEVEN OF SPADES (health) you will be heartsick over an enemy's jealousy, slander, or unfair play; or any underhandedness from relatives or would-be friends.

House of Inquirer

Heart Suit

ACE OF HEARTS (the abode) in the House of Inquirer indicates that you have a good home or will build a home to your liking; or a home condition has a great influence in your life.

KING OF HEARTS (enjoyment) there should be, or will be, some kindly person in your life who has your welfare at heart. This is a very good card to fall personally to you.

QUEEN OF HEARTS (friends) a friend will be of great influence in your life and will stand ready to help you.

JACK OF HEARTS (popularity) popularity will have something to do with your future, or you will receive plenty of publicity. You have fine prospects before you.

TEN OF HEARTS (marriage or union) if you are single, you will be married soon. If married but separated from your mate, a happy reunion; or a reunion with someone from a distance; or a happy marriage.

NINE OF HEARTS (your wish) your wish is very personal and you should get it very soon. You may have to overcome some obstacles first.

EIGHT OF HEARTS (moon-love) your future life should be full of love, even if your past has been full of sorrow.

SEVEN OF HEARTS (happiness) your future should be full of happiness, either through achieving something or through a talent of your own. Happiness is in store for you.

> When wealth is lost, nothing is lost;
> When health is lost, something is lost;
> When character is lost, all is lost.

> —Unknown
> motto on wall of a school in Germany

Diamond Suit

ACE OF DIAMONDS (new undertaking) you will go into a new undertaking, or one will be offered to you. Change of condition here in the immediate future; change for the best.

KING OF DIAMONDS (legal papers) you will have papers to sign; or be faced with a court action; or a professional man will play an important part in your life. If young and wondering what you should study, indicates a professional work of some kind should be to your benefit. Select one you would like best.

QUEEN OF DIAMONDS (seasons) time affects your personal affairs; you are waiting for something to happen or develop. Also old folks have something to do with your personal life. Things will change for you before the next season has passed. A big change for you.

JACK OF DIAMONDS (letters) a letter or news of some kind is coming to you; perhaps something connected with your work. Answer your mail promptly.

TEN OF DIAMONDS (money) you should receive a large sum of money soon. Money and investments indicated.

NINE OF DIAMONDS (surprises) you will have one of the biggest surprises of your life very soon.

EIGHT OF DIAMONDS (inheritance) an inheritance is coming to you soon, a gift—no one needs to die for you to receive this; or a small sum of money.

SEVEN OF DIAMONDS (success) your future holds success in a financial way. Remember not success in all things, but success in money matters.

Club Suit

ACE OF CLUBS (gift) recently you have received, or you will receive soon, a beautiful gift.

KING OF CLUBS (vocation) if in business, you will have much work; if working, a good position is yours; you will prosper.

QUEEN OF CLUBS (inquirer) you will never want; through loving friends or relatives you will be protected; also indicates you are capable of supporting yourself. Good life in old age indicated.

JACK OF CLUBS (relatives) some relative comes to live with you; or if you have children, they love to be with you and will never desert you.

TEN OF CLUBS (journey) you are facing a journey or change of conditions; a change for the better.

NINE OF CLUBS (luck) good luck is in store for you in all personal dealings. Use this luck.

EIGHT OF CLUBS (achievement) if you are working, you can expect good business; or something betters your source of livelihood; better financial conditions. If a dressmaker or designer, you will have a fine clientele.

SEVEN OF CLUBS (messages) if your wish pertains to a personal letter or message, you will surely receive it; an important message of some kind.

> Let each man think himself an act of God,
> His mind a thought, life a breath of God;
> And let each try, by great thoughts and good deeds,
> To show the most of Heaven he hath in him.

—P. J. Bailey

Spade Suit

ACE OF SPADES (death) you have lost someone you love dearly; or worry over a home condition; concentrate and clear up this condition.

KING OF SPADES (callers) someone will call who truly is a bore or some-one you don't care to see. This indicates a call you would like to avoid, but caller will arrive.

QUEEN OF SPADES (gratitude) some person pretends to be your friend—a woman. Watch for this person.

JACK OF SPADES (compass-thoughts) someone will try to gain your con-fidence through flattery; look out for a new acquaintance for their inten-tions are not right; or goodwill talk on the air.

TEN OF SPADES (sun) you will make a change of some real estate. A sale of something is indicated. The sun will shine here for you. If you sell real estate, a big deal soon.

NINE OF SPADES (disappointment) you are due for a disappointment, big loss, or you have just had one. Sometimes a big loss means a bigger gain; fate shapes things in a funny way. A delay indicated.

EIGHT OF SPADES (trouble) you have had some trouble or will have some; or you worry over troubles. Concentrate and don't worry. Grasp troubles firmly like nettles so that they cannot sting you.

SEVEN OF SPADES (health) you can overcome an illness through right thinking if you are ill; think healthy thoughts; we were never intended to be sick. You will be blessed with good health.

House of Luck

Heart Suit

ACE OF HEARTS (the abode) in the House of Luck indicates that you have good luck where you are now residing; or a home condition has something to do with your luck; or good luck in finding a home.

KING OF HEARTS (enjoyment) you will enjoy good luck through the wisdom of a true friend.

QUEEN OF HEARTS (friends) you have good friends who bring you good luck. The vibrations of some people bring good luck.

JACK OF HEARTS (popularity) you are lucky in being well thought of. Cultivate this. If a designer, you will design for the movies or famous people.

TEN OF HEARTS (marriage or union) luck is in store for you through your own wedding, and if married through the marriage of someone else. It also indicates luck in uniting business with pleasure.

NINE OF HEARTS (your wish) through luck you should get your wish, and soon.

EIGHT OF HEARTS (moon-love) you should be lucky in love.

SEVEN OF HEARTS (happiness) luck and happiness will come your way.

> *Good luck she is never a lady*
> *But the cursedest queen alive!*
> *Tricksey, wincing and jady,*
> *Kittle to lead or drive.*
> *Greet her—she's hailing a stranger!*
> *Meet her—she's busking to leave.*
> *Let her alone for a Shrew to the bone,*
> *And the hussy comes plucking your sleeve!*
>
> —Rudyard Kipling

Diamond Suit

ACE OF DIAMONDS (new undertaking) if you are contemplating a new venture, you should be very lucky with it; luck here plays a good part in what your future venture holds.

KING OF DIAMONDS (legal papers) through luck you will find a paper you lost or misplaced; or you will be lucky in retaining a paper you thought worthless and when a settlement is made you will profit by same; luck in papers here or a court action.

QUEEN OF DIAMONDS (seasons) this season should be one of luck to you; profit by this luck, as luck fades with time.

JACK OF DIAMONDS (letters) you will be lucky in keeping a certain letter that you intend to throw away; or you will be informed of some good luck through the mail; something like earning money or merchandise.

TEN OF DIAMONDS (money) you will be lucky in some money venture; like playing stock exchange, lottery or a gamble of some kind. This is good only for ten days at this reading.

NINE OF DIAMONDS (surprises) you will be surprised at some good fortune you will have in the very near future.

EIGHT OF DIAMONDS (inheritance) through luck you will win or inherit some money; or an old debt paid; or a gift of money. Steady income indicated.

SEVEN OF DIAMONDS (success) through a lucky strike on your part success comes to you, like in mining; something connected with the earth or soil.

Club Suit

ACE OF CLUBS (gift) you should be lucky in receiving gifts; lucky in gambles. A new proposition will be offered that is good.

KING OF CLUBS (vocation) you will get a good position through good luck; or good luck attends whatever your work is now.

QUEEN OF CLUBS (inquirer) you should have good luck for some time to come. Luck is with you.

JACK OF CLUBS (relatives) you and a relative or close friend will make a lucky investment through a ticket of chance; financial gains.

TEN OF CLUBS (journey) you have good luck through a change of residence, employment, or by a trip; a change for the better.

NINE OF CLUBS (luck) things should run smoothly for some time to come as this is a positive sign, an omen of good luck, when this card and house come together.

EIGHT OF CLUBS (achievement) through business connections you will profit; something meets with luck to your advantage.

SEVEN OF CLUBS (messages) a message or call puts you in a lucky situation; watch for this and use it to good advantage.

> *He that leaveth nothing to chance will do few things ill, but he will do very few things.*
>
> —Lord Halifax

Spade Suit

ACE OF SPADES (death) through a death some good luck will come to you. It betters your financial condition, like an inheritance; or you get a position vacated by death.

KING OF SPADES (callers) luck has something to do with a caller—they tell you about a good investment, or that you have won something; or you find out something to your benefit.

QUEEN OF SPADES (gratitude) for some good luck you have you will be very grateful to the person who helped you; or you will find something that belongs to someone else and be rewarded for returning it.

JACK OF SPADES (compass-thoughts) there is someone who will envy some good luck you will have. But remember good luck seems to follow only those who deserve it. Say every day, "I'm a lucky person"—it will bring a good vibration.

TEN OF SPADES (sun) some good fortune will come to you late in the afternoon. Watch for this—something you least expect.

NINE OF SPADES (disappointment) you will be disappointed in gambling, games of chance, or something you were hoping to win. Or a delay that turns out in your favor—a good luck delay.

EIGHT OF SPADES (trouble) you will bring some bad luck to yourself through being careless. Take care of your purse—someone might be helping himself; or your forget your change when you make a purchase.

SEVEN OF SPADES (health) you should guard your health; if ill, you will recover soon; or you will continue to have good health. Good luck and good health indicated.

House of Sun

Heart Suit

ACE OF HEARTS (the abode) in the House of Sun indicates that you will improve your garden if you have one; or buy new curtains for the windows or something for the home or outdoor living. Perhaps a patio party is indicated.

KING OF HEARTS (enjoyment) you should spend plenty of time outdoors. Walk, garden, if you can; get a sunsuit and wear it in the summer. You will get great enjoyment from the benefit you will receive.

QUEEN OF HEARTS (friends) the sun should shine in your life; also you will find the bluebird in your own backyard. Smile, be happy—it pays.

JACK OF HEARTS (popularity) for professional people, the House of Sun represents bright lights, brilliant career; the sun should break through for you soon.

TEN OF HEARTS (marriage or union) for married people, your life should be full of sunshine as years go by. Remember, in all lives a little rain must fall. If single, and you contemplate marriage, it should be a happy one.

NINE OF HEARTS (your wish) the sun should shine upon your wish. Look for news concerning it in the evening.

EIGHT OF HEARTS (moon-love) this is the house of sweethearts. Be kind, be true. If married, be cooperative with your mate. If single, you are greatly admired. Be sincere.

SEVEN OF HEARTS (happiness) there is great happiness in store for you during the summer months. Vacation and a happy home life.

Spring is with us once again
With bursting buds and flowers
We hate to lose you like a friend
Time measures pleasant hours.

—Margarete Ward

Diamond Suit

ACE OF DIAMONDS (new undertaking) the sun should bless all those that farm—for this house is for new planting. Things that grow good crops indicated. For others, plenty on the table.

KING OF DIAMONDS (legal papers) this house belongs to those in the professional world—doctors, lawyers, etc. If a judge, you will be called upon to render a hard decision; or sunshine in your life by a just decision if in court.

QUEEN OF DIAMONDS (seasons) the next three months the sun should shine brightly for you.

JACK OF DIAMONDS (letters) sunshine through hasty news, letters, messages indicated.

TEN OF DIAMONDS (money) there will be some object like jewelry bought by you or for you; also could be money resulting from work in the ground like mining or oil.

NINE OF DIAMONDS (surprises) a good surprise awaits you tonight.

EIGHT OF DIAMONDS (inheritance) the sun will shine for you either through a larger income or an inheritance. Concentrate and know a better condition awaits you.

SEVEN OF DIAMONDS (success) sunshine in your life and success. That is enough.

> *Bring back the singing; and the scent*
> *Of meadowlands at dewy prime;*
> *Oh, bring again my heart's content,*
> *Thou Spirit of the Summertime!*

—William Allingham, *Song*

Club Suit

ACE OF CLUBS (gift) there will be something given you that should bring sunshine into your life—like a pet, a bird, a dog, horse, etc. Indicates something alive.

KING OF CLUBS (vocation) if you work indoors, do not neglect to walk and get out into the air. The sun is needed by you—or the sun will brighten your life by right living.

QUEEN OF CLUBS (inquirer) sunshine and happiness for you after the rain; but we must all have rain in our lives to balance the scales. Good times ahead.

JACK OF CLUBS (relatives) your relatives and friends bring sunshine to you; visit them, entertain them. If some have faults overlook them. None of us are perfect. Do not be petty; be bighearted.

TEN OF CLUBS (journey) be careful if your vacation is near water not to get too sunburned. Indicates a hunting trip, skiing party, skating or bob-sledding in the snow. Plenty of fun.

NINE OF CLUBS (luck) the sun should shine brightly in the future through luck. Say on arising each morning, "I am a lucky person just to be here on earth." Luck will vibrate to you.

EIGHT OF CLUBS (achievement) indicates happiness. Cheerful working companions or employees.

SEVEN OF CLUBS (messages) you will talk about a restaurant night club or phone messages about the purchase of same. A talk about a place that uses bright lights at night.

Spade Suit

ACE OF SPADES (death) you will speak of a deceased person. They are happy because you remember them.

KING OF SPADES (callers) this sun house is for any man in uniform; public service. It indicates constant change like the sun; one location one day, and on the high seas another. You seem to change like the sun.

QUEEN OF SPADES (gratitude) late in the evening you will discover a misplaced article, or someone will call and enlighten you on some subject. Constructive conversation.

JACK OF SPADES (compass-thoughts) as this house represents space, distance, etc., let your thoughts always be on the positive, constructive side. I detest a taunting guffaw over a purchase or anything else a person is trying to do. It may be only said in jest, but it is a ruinous vibration.

TEN OF SPADES (sun) your sun should rise high this year—especially if dealing in anything pertaining to the earth: land, mining, oil, crops, etc.

NINE OF SPADES (disappointment) the sun will shine though a delay. Do not be upset over this delay. Relax and wait. Time is your ally.

EIGHT OF SPADES (trouble) the sun coming into your life soon will erase all trouble. Concentrate on happy thoughts. Never say it cannot be done.

SEVEN OF SPADES (health) sunshine and health indicated. Get outdoor bath in the sunshine; get in tune with nature.

How to Find Your Soul Age By Numerology

The system I was taught to measure time by is based on the twelve calendar months, or the period of time that it takes to make a year such as 365 days, etc. This system has nothing to do with the houses or signs of the Zodiac, used in astrology, but pertains to our calendar year only, beginning with January as the first month.

There are nine numbers by which all calculations on this earth are made, beyond the number nine all are repetition. No matter how large a sum, it can be reduced to a single figure by simple addition.

To determine your soul number, write in one column the number of your birth month (January 1, February 2, etc.), the date, and the year.

EXAMPLE: Birth date January 23rd, 1935.

Birth Month	1
Birthday	23
Birth year	1935
Add together	1959

Now place these figures in a single row and add.	1
	9
	5
	9
Total	24

Add the figures of this total.	2
	4
	6

Your soul number is 6, or this is your sixth life here on earth.

DIRECTIONS: First find your soul age through numerology, as explained on the previous page. Then turn to the astrology section and find your birth month. Study your natural characteristics according to your birth sign, and find the vocation best suited for you according to your soul age and take advantage of what is predicted there for you.

A Lesson in Astrology

An accurate horoscope is usually based upon the date, year, and hour of one's birth. It is my purpose to help the reader to ascertain his soul age, or the number of times he has lived on earth, as this has a vast influence in determining the extent to which he can take advantage of the knowledge gained from his horoscope.

People are often puzzled by the fact that, though their horoscopes accurately describe their characteristics, they yet do not succeed in achieving the thing for which they seemed destined. For instance, one will say, "My stars tell me I should be a great poet. I love poetry above everything else, but I can't write a line." This is due to the fact that these puzzled people are young souls. Their hopes and aspirations have taken shape, but they are not yet old enough in experience to have attained their goals, and if they will continue striving, they will achieve much in this life and build a solid foundation for the next life and each successive life will bring them nearer to their heart's desire. After all, there are more successful people than failures in this world.

You may say, "If my character, my surroundings, and all the events of my life are determined in advance by the stars under which I was born, what is the use of my trying to do anything about it? I cannot change the stars."

That is true. You cannot change the laws of nature, but you can make use of them. All the universe, from the smallest flower to the farthest star, is governed by natural laws which we cannot change. But there is another truth which we must also take into account, and that is the nature of man. The thing which distinguishes man from all the other animals is his desire for and his power to acquire knowledge, and by this knowledge of the natural laws he is enabled to harness the forces of nature and cause them to serve him. For example, suppose I have brushed an expensive vase off the table. The laws of gravity cause the vase to fall, and it would be shattered, but I reach out quickly and catch the vase before it strikes the floor. I have not broken the law of gravity; the law still operates, but

my knowledge of that law has made it possible for me to forestall its natural consequences.

So the knowledge of the influences which govern one's destiny may be used in planning one's life. If we know that certain conditions or tendencies will prevail at certain stages of our lives, we can conduct ourselves in such a way as to take advantage of favorable conditions and be on guard against those which are unfavorable.

Many persons born the same day, year, and month, even to the hour and minute, are very different from each other. The reason is that some have been born more than once in the same month of the year, or under the same planet, and have therefore developed to a high degree the characteristics of that sign. That is why we see one man prosperous, living up to the best in his horoscope, while another is struggling for a bare existence. Experiences in one life are carried over into the next, like overflowing harmonics, as in music, or an octave higher in the same key, adding to our knowledge and power. It is true that one person may leave fame and fortune behind him in a first life here, but we do not know what he has done on another planet before he came here, while another must be born again and again before he arrives at his goal. But no matter what line of endeavor we follow, each of us is a part of the scheme of things here, even if only in a small way. As everything is worked out in harmony, for concentrated harmonious thought and action are the key to success. This would be a very unjust world, with one person prospering and another in want, if each were not given another life in which to balance the account.

As we learn more and more to understand the planetary influences which govern the lives of human beings, it will become easier to guide and direct children in the line of their natural characteristics. In the schools today, educators study the toys a child likes to play with in order to find out what he will be best fitted for as he grows up. If they had a horoscope made for the child, they would not have to waste time in studying him at play; they would know what toys to give him to help him develop his talents.

Every mother should realize that each child is an individual soul, placed in her care for the betterment of her own soul as well as that of the

child. She should keep a correct record of his birth—hour, minute, etc.—and have a chart of life made at once for her guidance in raising this child. Then she would understand her child and there would not be that conflict which is so common between mothers and their children. She would know what each child likes and dislikes and could cater to her children's happiness as well as her own, and also be able to start them on a useful career early in life, for their natural characteristics would be revealed to her.

A person born under a different planet each time is a well-rounded individual, is usually a world traveler in his seventh, eighth, or ninth life here on earth. He is well versed in almost every subject, learns easily, retains what he learns, and is, as a rule, a very wholesome, powerful person who is recognized at once as such. The Aura, or light, that surrounds an old soul of this type is very powerful. His presence is felt the minute he enters a room. We can feel the Aura, or power in learning, which this person possesses, the minute we meet him.

Each house, or sign of the Zodiac, is divided into three periods of approximately ten days each. For example, the first period of the second house, Taurus, runs from April 21st to May 2nd. Here there is an overflow of planetary influences from the first house, Aries, into the second house, Taurus. Those born in this period are susceptible to the influences of Aries as well as Taurus, and the nearer the birth date lies to April 21st, or the cusp, the more pronounced will be the characteristics of Aries. Anyone born near the cusp of his sign, or when one sign is changing to another (from the 21st of one month to the 1st of the next) should study the general characteristics of the preceding sign. One born in this period of any month can rise to the highest in anything he chooses if he will apply himself and develop his possibilities, for he has the influence of both signs to help him, but he must also be on his guard against the unfavorable influences of both houses. So, if you are born between the cusp and the first of any month, strive for higher things. Your planets and stars will double help you.

From the 2nd to the 10th of any month, the native has lesser vibrations of planetary influences of the preceding sign, and from the 10th to the cusp (19th, 20th, or 21st of any month, whichever the cusp falls on) he has the most forceful planetary influences of his sign governing him. If

you are an old soul, you will make the most of any period of the month in which you were born.

My Chinese teacher taught me that the stars only guide your destiny, like a lamp that guides you down a dark path. The light may be ever so bright, but if you shut your eyes, of what use is the light? Your stars predict your natural characteristics; it is up to you to find which vocation you like best and specialize in it. Then watch your stars light your way. If we make the most of each life, each subsequent life becomes easier, and if we fail, the next life will be harder. We should endeavor to live a useful, good life, so that we will not have to work out a Karma, or retribution, in our next life.

Study your natural characteristics according to your birth month, sign, and soul age and take advantage of what is predicted for you. As you gain knowledge, you will develop your natural characteristics, and may do many things during your life that are predicted for you. Remember, you can only get out of the predictions the good things that you work for and concentrate on, for the stars will not drop them into your lap. "He who hesitates is lost." TRY!

Though my soul may set in darkness,
it will rise in perfect light,
I have loved the stars too fondly
to be fearful of the night.

—Unknown

Aries

The Ram

March 22 to April 20

Ruled by Mars. First House of the Zodiac. (Fire)

Aries people have forceful personalities and great executive ability. They are ambitious and industrious as well as generous and idealistic. They are great starters, but are inclined to leave things unfinished, and they should guard against a tendency to become obstinate.

MARRIAGE: Partners for marriage or business should be chosen from the same sign (Aries) or from Leo (July 24 to August 23) or Sagittarius (November 23 to December 22).

HEALTH: Ailments to guard against are head injuries, stomach or kidney ailments, paralysis, and apoplexy.

BIRTHSTONE: Sapphire. If you do not care for your birthstone, wear a diamond instead, for it indicates purity and gives strength.

VOCATIONS:

Soul Age 1, 2, or 3	*Soul Age 4, 5, or 6*	*Soul Age 7, 8, or 9*
Military	Mechanic	Chemist
Nanny	Department Manager	Musician
Sailor	Dentist	Doctor
School Supervisor	Clothier	Singer
Police Force	Military Officer	Executive
Playground Supervisor	Dental Assistant	Florist
Fireman	Computer Technician	Banker
Clerk	Office Assistant	Storekeeper
Waiter		Computer Programmer
Office Supervisor		

Taurus

The Bull

April 21 to May 21

Ruled by Venus. Second House of the Zodiac. (Earth)

Taurus people are calm and self-controlled. They are home lovers, are fond of children, and enjoy creature comforts. They are quiet but forceful, undemonstrative but loyal. Taurus people are not the romantic lovers, but they make faithful mates and affectionate parents.

The Taurian is an earth child and should seek a vocation closely associated with the earth. Taurians love music and may become great singers or speakers or radio announcers.

MARRIAGE: Partners for marriage or business should be chosen from the same sign (Taurus) or from Virgo (August 24 to September 23) or Capricorn (December 23 to January 20).

HEALTH: Ailments to guard against are edema, diseases of the kidneys, throat, and generative system. Avoid rich foods, wines, etc.

BIRTHSTONE: Emerald. If you do not care for your birthstone, wear a diamond instead, for it indicates purity and gives strength.

VOCATIONS:

Soul Age 1, 2, or 3	Soul Age 4, 5, or 6	Soul Age 7, 8, or 9
Farmer	Machine Operator	Landlord
Chicken Farmer	Service Station Operator	Weaver
Cattle Rancher		Oil Rigger
Dog Trainer	Dry Goods	Miner
Lumberman	Manufacturer	Nurse
Housecleaner	Wine Maker	Steel Worker
	Produce Dealer	Potter
	Florist	Cheese Maker
	Computer Repair	Gardener

Gemini

The Twins

May 22 to June 21

Ruled by Mercury. Third House of the Zodiac. (Air)

People born under Gemini, The Twins, are often torn between two sides of their character. They are changeable, or "mercurial," as the name of their planet suggests, but they are charming and often brilliant. They are best adapted to vocations which call for mental facility. They are apt to scatter their forces, and should cultivate the ability to concentrate.

MARRIAGE: Partners for marriage or business should be chosen from the same sign (Gemini) or from Libra (September 24 to October 23) or Aquarius (January 21 to February 19).

HEALTH: Ailments to guard against are diseases of the lungs or the blood and abdominal operations.

BIRTHSTONE: Agate. If you do not care for your birthstone, wear a diamond instead, for it indicates purity and gives strength.

VOCATIONS:

Soul Age 1, 2, or 3	*Soul Age 4, 5, or 6*	*Soul Age 7, 8, or 9*
Restaurant Owner	Dancer	Artist
Beautician	Office Associate	Musician
Hotel Manager	Sales Manager	Venture Capitalist
Cashier	Bookkeeper	Advertising
Bank Cashier	Office Manager	Chemist
Dietician	File Clerk	Professor of Languages
Head Waiter	Musician	Doctor
Career Counselor	Teacher	Dance Instructor
	Web Designer	

Cancer

The Crab

June 22 to July 23

Ruled by the Moon. Fourth House of the Zodiac. (Water)

Cancer people are sensitive and given to worry. When this sensitiveness is controlled, it makes its possessor adaptable and charming; when uncontrolled, it leads to morbid introspection and misunderstandings. Cancer people can be influenced by sympathy and kindness but cannot be driven. They are constant in their affection.

MARRIAGE: Partners for marriage or business should be chosen from the same sign (Cancer) or from Scorpio (October 24 to November 22) or Pisces (February 20 to March 21).

HEALTH: Ailments to guard against are rheumatism, gout, poor circulation, lung trouble.

BIRTHSTONE: Ruby. If you do not care for your birthstone, wear a diamond instead, for it indicates purity and gives strength.

VOCATIONS:

Soul Age 1, 2, or 3	*Soul Age 4, 5, or 6*	*Soul Age 7, 8, or 9*
Sales Manager	Sales Clerk	Importer
Postal Worker	Billing Clerk	Perfume Manufacturer
Chef	Railroad Engineer	Traveling Salesperson
Receptionist	Housekeeper	Wine Merchant
Fisherman	Truck Driver	Naval Career
File Clerk	Computer Assembler	Cosmetic Merchant
		Traffic Manager
		Food Service Manager

Leo

The Lion

July 24 to August 23

Ruled by the Sun. Fifth House of the Zodiac. (Fire)

Leo people are born leaders, industrious, energetic, and magnetic. Their love of power and authority, unless properly controlled, tends to make them domineering. However, they are generous and loyal and seldom harbor grudges. They have a strong desire to be looked up to, and usually deserve to be.

MARRIAGE: Partners for marriage or business should be chosen from the same sign (Leo) or from Sagittarius (November 23 to December 22) or Aries (March 22 to April 20).

HEALTH: Ailments to guard against are rheumatism and diseases of the heart, liver, and spleen.

BIRTHSTONE: Sardonyx. If you do not care for your birthstone, wear a diamond instead, for it indicates purity and gives strength.

VOCATIONS:

Soul Age 1, 2, or 3	*Soul Age 4, 5, or 6*	*Soul Age 7, 8, or 9*
Miner	Supervisor	Geologist
Dry Cleaner	Nurse	Florist
Plumber	Military Officer	Office Manager
Kindergarten Teacher	Office Assistant	Hospital Administrator
Carpenter	Teacher	Jeweler
Construction Worker	Beautician	Writer
Stone Mason	Sales	Landscape Architect
	Data Entry	School Principal

Virgo

The Virgin

August 24 to September 23

Ruled by Mercury. Sixth House of the Zodiac. (Earth)

Virgo people are ruled by intellect rather than emotion. They are inventive, analytical, and critical; in fact, they are apt to be overcritical, both of themselves and others. They are versatile, gifted in conversation and repartee. They work unselfishly for others but need to cultivate the gift of tolerance.

MARRIAGE: Partners for marriage or business should be chosen from the same sign (Virgo) or from Capricorn (December 23 to January 20) or Taurus (April 21 to May 21).

HEALTH: Ailments to guard against are ulcers and diseases of the stomach and nervous system.

BIRTHSTONE: Chrysolite. If you do not care for your birthstone, wear a diamond instead, for it indicates purity and gives strength.

VOCATIONS:

Soul Age 1, 2, or 3	*Soul Age 4, 5, or 6*	*Soul Age 7, 8, or 9*
Bookkeeper	Law Clerk	Lawyer
Assistant	Court Clerk	Judge
Bank Teller	Real Estate Broker	Court Clerk
Delivery Specialist	Court Stenographer	Real Estate Broker
	Builder	Writer
	Accountant	Professor of English
	Draftsman	Professor of Languages
	Designer	Computer Analyst
	Web Designer	

Libra

The Balance

September 24 to October 23

Ruled by Venus. Seventh House of the Zodiac. (Air)

Libra people are lovers of beauty. They hate all sham and deceit, crudeness or grossness, not because it is wrong but because it is ugly. They are honest and generous, socially gifted and delightful companions. They hesitate to assume the responsibilities of marriage, but are steadfast in their affections.

MARRIAGE: Partners for marriage or business should be chosen from the same sign (Libra) or from Gemini (May 22 to June 21) or Aquarius (January 21 to February 19).

HEALTH: Ailments to guard against are diseases of the stomach, kidneys, nerves, and skin.

BIRTHSTONE: Opal. If you do not care for your birthstone, wear a diamond instead, for it indicates purity and gives strength.

VOCATIONS:

Soul Age 1, 2, or 3	*Soul Age 4, 5, or 6*	*Soul Age 7, 8, or 9*
Landscape Gardener	Mechanical Engineer	Doctor
Tailor	Clothing Designer	Writer
Electrician	Architect	Sculptor
Interior Decorator	Music Teacher	Actor
Painter	Interior Decorator	Play Producer
Florist	Art Dealer	Artist
Carpenter	Musician	Art Collector
Housecleaner	Web Designer	
Mechanic		
Sales		

Scorpio ♏

The Scorpion

October 24 to November 22

Ruled by Mars. Eighth House of the Zodiac. (Water)

Scorpio people are characterized by a driving force which overcomes all obstacles. They are capable of passionate devotion to a cause or a person, but must guard against excess and folly in matters pertaining to love. They are shrewd and analytical, strong yet subtle. They should cultivate a sympathetic understanding of those about them.

MARRIAGE: Partners for marriage or business should be chosen from the same sign (Scorpio) or from Cancer (June 22 to July 23) or Pisces (February 20 to March 21).

HEALTH: Ailments to guard against are gland trouble, diseases of the bowels and generative system.

BIRTHSTONE: Topaz. If you do not care for your birthstone, wear a diamond instead, for it indicates purity and gives strength.

VOCATIONS:

Soul Age 1, 2, or 3	Soul Age 4, 5, or 6	Soul Age 7, 8, or 9
Draftsman	Lawyer	Pharmacist
Designer	Writer	Actor
Produce Dealer	Chemist	Publisher
Music Teacher	Perfume Manufacturer	Writer
School Teacher	Auctioneer	Advertiser
Nurse	Interior Decorator	Singer
	Computer Programmer	Outdoors Guide
		Composer

Sagittarius

The Archer

November 23 to December 22

Ruled by Jupiter. Ninth House of the Zodiac. (Fire)

Sagittarius people are honest, fearless, and unselfish. They have keen insight and intuition, are frank and direct, but inclined to be too brusque. In matters of the heart they are so fastidious that they sometimes appear cold. They are appreciated where understood and they make excellent partners in either business or marriage.

MARRIAGE: Partners for marriage or business should be chosen from the same sign (Sagittarius) or from Leo (July 24 to August 23) or Aries (March 22 to April 20).

HEALTH: Ailments to guard against are colds, bronchitis, and diseases of the liver and blood.

BIRTHSTONE: Turquoise. If you do not care for your birthstone, wear a diamond instead, for it indicates purity and gives strength.

VOCATIONS:

Soul Age 1, 2, or 3	*Soul Age 4, 5, or 6*	*Soul Age 7, 8, or 9*
Divinity Student	Mechanical Engineer	Travel Writer
Surveyor	Clergyman	Prison Administrator
Lecturer	Construction Engineer	Religious Publisher
Singer	Divinity Professor	Philanthropist
Radio/TV Broadcaster	Inventor	Journalist
Chemical Laboratory Assistant	Actor	Theologian
Computer Support	Writer	Magazine Publisher
	Musician	Healer

Capricorn ♑

The Goat

December 23 to January 20

Ruled by Saturn. Tenth House of the Zodiac. (Earth)

Capricorn people are distinguished by ambition and by the ability to stick to an undertaking until they achieve success. They are hard workers, practical, and very independent. They have magnetic personalities but are cautious in matters of love. A Capricorn person never falls in love until he is sure that his love is returned.

MARRIAGE: Partners for marriage or business should be chosen from the same sign (Capricorn) or from Taurus (April 21 to May 21) or Virgo (August 24 to September 23).

HEALTH: Ailments to guard against are ulcers, diseases of the bladder, gall bladder, and digestive organs.

BIRTHSTONE: Garnet. If you do not care for your birthstone, wear a diamond instead, for it indicates purity and gives strength.

VOCATIONS:

Soul Age 1, 2, or 3	*Soul Age 4, 5, or 6*	*Soul Age 7, 8, or 9*
Sales	School Teacher	Advertising Executive
Department Manager	Music Teacher	Lawyer
Retail Buyer	Bookkeeper	Doctor
Merchant	Office Assistant	Minister
Store Owner	Bank Clerk	Public Speaker
	Chemist	
	Geneticist	

Aquarius

The Water Bearer

January 21 to February 19

Ruled by Uranus. Eleventh House of the Zodiac. (Air)

Aquarius people are quiet and reserved, modest and unselfish. They give freely of their talents for the good of others. They view life impersonally but are loyal friends. They are gifted and frequently rise to fame. Aquarius people have a mental poise which gives them power over circumstances, and they should rely on their own judgment rather than that of others.

MARRIAGE: Partners for marriage or business should be chosen from the same sign (Aquarius) or from Gemini (May 22 to June 21) or Libra (September 24 to October 23).

HEALTH: Ailments to guard against are poor circulation, anemia, heart trouble, and diseases of the bladder and kidneys.

BIRTHSTONE: Amethyst. If you do not care for your birthstone, wear a diamond instead, for it indicates purity and gives strength.

VOCATIONS:

Soul Age 1, 2, or 3	*Soul Age 4, 5, or 6*	*Soul Age 7, 8, or 9*
Nurse	Writer	Dentist
Butcher	Chemist	Doctor
Chef	Doctor	Undertaker
Baker	Dentist	Lawyer
Beautician	Laboratory Technician	
Haircutter	Computer Programmer	

Pisces

The Fishes

February 20 to March 21

Ruled by Jupiter and Neptune. Twelfth House of the Zodiac. (Water)

Pisces people are apt to be very popular. They are generous and socially charming. They have fine instincts and high ambitions but are handicapped by indecision. They should cultivate the habit of weighing the pros and cons of a question, choosing a course of action, and then standing by it, no matter what obstacles they meet.

MARRIAGE: Partners for marriage or business should be chosen from the same sign (Pisces) or from Cancer (June 22 to July 23) or Scorpio (October 24 to November 22).

HEALTH: Ailments to guard against are nervous disorders, consumption, tumors, and paralysis.

BIRTHSTONE: Bloodstone. If you do not care for your birthstone, wear a diamond instead, for it indicates purity and gives strength.

VOCATIONS:

Soul Age 1, 2, or 3	Soul Age 4, 5, or 6	Soul Age 7, 8, or 9
Stone Mason	Play Producer	Playwright
Carpenter	Choreographer	Actor
Machinist	Advertising	Theatre
Electrician	Actor	Singer
Designer	Builder	Musician
Computer Programmer	Writer	Theatrical Designer
	Architect	Dancer
	Interior Decorator